Beauty Beyond Words

Dr Lionel Dakers is one of the leading church musicians of our day. His eventful career has included posts at Eton College, St George's Chapel Windsor, Ripon and Exeter Cathedrals, and culminated in his becoming Director of the Royal School of Church Music from 1972–89.

He served as President of the Royal College of Organists and as a member of the Archbishops' Commission on Church Music, and was awarded a CBE in 1983.

His many published books include *Places Where They Sing* and *A Handbook of Parish Music*. He lives in Salisbury.

Beauty Beyond Words

Enriching worship through music

Lionel Dakers

CANTERBURY
PRESS
Norwich

© Lionel Dakers 2000

First published in 2000
by The Canterbury Press Norwich
(a publishing imprint of Hymns Ancient & Modern
Limited a registered charity)
St Mary's Works, St Mary's Plain
Norwich, Norfolk NR3 3BH

British Library Cataloguing in Publication Data

A catalogue record for this book is available
from the British Library

ISBN 1-85311-351-4

Typeset by Rowland Phototypesetting Ltd,
Bury St Edmunds, Suffolk
Music typeset by Halstan & Co. Ltd,
Amersham, Buckinghamshire
and printed in Great Britain by Biddles Ltd,
Guildford and King's Lynn

I will sing with the spirit, and I will sing with the
understanding also.
I Corinthians 14:15

Singing is speech beautified.
Edward C. Bairstow, Singing Learned From Speech

Bad art is a great deal worse than no art at all.
Oscar Wilde

Contents

I

Introduction

Most acts of public worship rely heavily on the use of music. The power it exerts to enrich, detract from, impoverish or even destroy worship emphasizes its significance and its influence. Nor are any faults always those of the music as such, but sometimes those of the people performing it. Music and its performance has an impact on the worshipper for better or for worse.

The reasons why this should be so have encouraged me to write this book which will seek to suggest, frequently through example, how our worship can be raised to the heights through music, be we performers or listeners. This involves both visionary thinking and logical planning.

Music in worship, as in secular song, has one specific objective, that of elevating words by carrying them a stage further, and a significant stage at that. Ideally, the fusion of words and music should enhance our devotions, our contemplation, and therefore our worship. This is the object of music in worship. The words usually give birth to the music, one of the exceptions being Francis Jackson's hymn tune EAST ACKLAM which inspired Fred Pratt Green to write the words of the harvest hymn 'For the fruits of his creation'. And a number of recent hymns, particularly from Iona, are sung to traditional Scottish tunes.

Earlier this century Sir Edward Bairstow, the eminent organist of York Minster, likened choral music to 'speech beautified', as later did Herbert Howells who 'knew very well the power of music to influence and persuade, and it begins where the spoken word leaves off'.[1] Music has an extraordinary influence on worship. For centuries past the amalgam of words linked with music has exerted a significant effect on public worship patterns, irrespective of geographical or denominational boundaries. It is no exaggeration to suggest that hymnody speaks a common language which binds denominations together in a unique way. This is something we have by and large failed to seize on as an instrument of ecumenism, and this despite the fact that the hymns of the Wesleys, the Roman Catholic Cardinal Newman and others are freely shared by the denominations. Certain hymns emphasize this, notably 'Thy hand, O God, has guided' where each verse ends with the proclamation 'One Church, one faith, one Lord'. Another salient example is Bishop George Bell's great hymn 'Christ is the King!' which is shot through with a longing for unity and reaches a climax with its all-enveloping parting cry 'and the whole Church at last be one'.

In this book I try to spell out in some detail specific examples where music has elevated texts as well as identifying some instances where it has done the very opposite. There are suggestions for choir directors, choirs, organists and instrumentalists towards achieving the best possible in performance to the advantage of the worshipper in the pew. Church musicians owe this to congregations, realizing the influence they exert through their singing and playing of hymns more than in anthems and motets which, after all, are the icing on the cake. Whether or not they realize this, and willingly subscribe to it, or whether they view hymns as a perfunctory chore, is another matter. Surveying the current hymn scene from parish church to cathedral is not always the edifying prospect it ought to be, simply because we all too often encounter apathy and a lack of imagination in what is relayed to those on the receiving end. To use a contemporary phrase, hymns are put on the back burner.

From earliest times the Church was quick to seize on what the fusion of two art forms could achieve through this interlock of words and music; for most of us song is germane as an expression of whatever our emotions may happen to be at any one time. This process has continued down through the centuries as a major ingredient in worship, although inevitably some examples are more highly charged and inspired than others, for sometimes the music fails to match up to the words. And, if the music is either uninspired or grammatically deficient there is little anyone can do, even though some hymns in this category happen to be among those which are the best loved.

We need to remind ourselves also that the aural aspect of worship can for many be equated with the visual, a rich and equally potent ingredient in worship for those who wish to contemplate through the eye the church in which they find themselves. The combination of the aural and the visual is valued by many, though we must equally respect those who find sight and sound, especially when savouring of the ornate, a distraction or even a deterrent rather than an aid to contemplation. The functional architecture of some non-conformist churches bears this out, with the ultimate being the Quaker approach to worship.

Broadly speaking, we shall consider the two main areas into which music in worship falls. First, hymns and those parts of the Eucharist involving the congregation. These are, *par excellence*, instances where the people have a rightful musical role to play. Whether there is a choir to give a lead does not matter, though if there is no choir the onus falls fairly and squarely on the congregation. The fact that some of us have difficulty in finding the note, and maybe resort to growling an octave or so lower than the music, is neither here nor there. It is right, and essential, for a congregation to participate fully at these moments and in doing so to express through song their emotions of joy, sadness, penitence, or whatever.

Song is one of the oldest ways of expressing sentiments, be it the haunting lyricism of age-old folk tunes such as GREENSLEEVES, WALY, WALY, and the LONDONDERRY AIR or, in our time, the seemingly never-failing lure of 'Top of the Pops' – though in this last instance there is precious little evidence of speech being beautified.

The Church's counterpart to secular folk music is plainsong which has an equally rewarding aura, though being somewhat austere it does not find universal acceptance. It is often construed as a High Church or Roman Catholic practice, though today it is neither exclusively. Even so, these sacred and secular elements run more or less in parallel and are well-proven examples of music of the people. A further responsibility for congregations is their role, again rightful, in singing at least the Creed in the Communion service, and in many parishes the Gloria.

There are, however, instances where the sacred and the secular become intertwined, and to good effect. Michael Tippett not only wrote the words for his oratorio *A Child of our Time* but then set them to music, and with especial success in the spirituals. These punctuate the main narrative in much the same way as Bach in his settings of the Passion story inserted chorales at certain points for the congregation to make their comment and reflection. Benjamin Britten's *War Requiem* is a further example, with the poignant war poems of Wilfred Owen integrated into the traditional text of the Requiem Mass. These instances, although they come outside our survey as such, are nevertheless outstanding examples of texts, and not always religious ones, being greatly beautified through the addition of music.

At this stage we might well pause to reflect further on this parallelism between sacred and secular music. Alongside

Bach's colossal output for the Church come, though later in time, the secular songs of Schubert, Brahms and Hugo Wolf, as examples of German poetry which each composer found rewarding, and inspiring, to set. Nearer to our time are those wonderfully haunting romantic melodies of Richard Strauss such as his opera *Der Rosenkavalier* and the *Four Last Songs*, nineteenth-century German romantic music to its very fingertips. These are but one or two random examples of this parallelism in which great poetry has triggered off the inspiration of composers. How much there is for church musicians to learn from secular music.

Although in the Church there are somewhat different factors, the object of the exercise is the same, for without the words there would not be the highly inspiring vocal music that we enjoy – the one subtle difference being that the secular is for entertainment. Nineteenth-century Europe was aglow with the 'Romantic' in every art form. The Church was no exception, though often, particularly in England, with a liberal injection of sentiment which at its worst is cloying and sugary *in excelsis*! Many of the anthems and service settings of this period, as we shall later see, are equally deficient and show scant evidence of inspiration; they are merely routine plodding, as off-putting to the performer as to the listener. Is it therefore any wonder that the continent, and Germany in particular, wrote off our small island as an isolated backwater, 'a land without music'? One of the few exceptions of this period was Mendelssohn who successfully contrived in his sacred music to produce eminently singable anthems, motets and oratorios which, by and large, have withstood the test of time and continue to be widely performed.

In the twentieth century there were composers such as Stanford, Parry, Elgar and Vaughan Williams writing as much for the Church as for other areas, and in doing so contriving to extract every ounce of possibility and vision in setting great texts, while employing the full palette of choral and orchestral resources. Elgar, for example, set Cardinal Newman's epic poem *The Dream of Gerontius*, while Vaughan Williams used equally impressive forces for the secular poetry of Walt Whitman in *A Sea Symphony*. If ever there was a thrilling example of word painting we need look no further than the opening bars, surely one of the most remarkable pictorial examples of what combined choral and orchestral forces can produce. Yet both these composers could write equally beautiful simple miniatures, Elgar with *Ave Verum Corpus* and Vaughan Williams in his magical *O taste and see*, first heard at the 1953 Coronation service and most effectively sandwiched between veritable giants such as Parry's *I was glad* and Handel's *Zadok the Priest*. Fine settings of the Te Deum (see page 74) include Vaughan Williams reacting in a quite different way in projecting a great text. Finally, and as something of an unusual hybrid, can be cited Verdi's *Requiem*, often seriously considered to be his best opera! To quote Bertram Barnby:

> Verdi shocked many people by writing his Requiem Mass in his own idiom – the stage. Who would have expected to hear Sanctus, Benedictus, and Hosanna swept along in a tripping fugal dance lasting less than three minutes? Here we have a great genius dedicating his talents to God and so giving us a glimpse of the worship of heaven that is original, exciting and inspiring – as I hope heaven will be.[2]

So far, in speaking in general terms of vocal music, it is often with an implied organ accompaniment, but today much more use is being made of instruments other than the organ. It is interesting, perhaps ironic, to realize that when the Oxford Movement came into being during the nineteenth century the village orchestra in the church gallery was dispensed with and in its place came the organ and a robed chair, all housed within the often confined space of a chancel. Today, with liturgical thinking tending to be focussed on a centrally positioned altar area with all concerned able to see and to be more easily involved, the choir, and even the organ, is sometimes being moved back again into the west gallery. Stinsford Church near Dorchester, the setting for the Mellstock choir in Hardy's *Far from the Madding Crowd*, has done just this, and to great advantage.

In evangelical and 'renewed' churches the organ has to a large extent been sidelined and instrumental groups substituted in its place. This, it is claimed, provides an opportunity for those with such skills to be actively involved in worship, though it is ironic that in many such instances this has come either through a lack of organists or, regrettably, because of the current vogue for many clergy to be resistent to traditional music. Although the supply of organists has to a considerable extent evaporated, the situation is not helped by the absence of job satisfaction. The current position is further eroded when some of the traditional musicians are past their sell-by date and so set in their ways that the music they produce can be routinely dull, though this does not excuse their un-Christian treatment by autocratic clergy and PCCs.

There are other dangers, notably when instrumentalists are encouraged willy-nilly to perform in church, however minimal their technique and skill. This can be counter-productive, the more so when the music is highly amplified, and maybe with a percussive 'rock' section. It is sometimes forgotten that people today demand high standards as much in the music they hear in church as in any other aspect of life. The oft-quoted wish to give people what they want, irrespective of any other considerations, can be a dangerous path to tread, as was the suggestion made to me by a clergyman that God is only being fully worshipped when the music is loud and fast. This aspect of contemporary worship will be addressed later, for some of what is on offer seems to have little relevance to the concept of beautifying speech through the addition of music.

Traditional church music, on the other hand, is not everyone's meat, restricted as it can be for congregations weaned on a fairly rigid diet of hymnody which can become distinctly wearisome when choir and organ plod on verse after verse, giving the impression that this is a boring routine which they all too readily wish to dispense with in exchange for more meaty fare such as anthems and motets. If choir and organist worship through their music, as they surely should, they must be fully involved in *all* things musical and not be selective as to what they like or dislike. The onus on the musicians is as considerable as it is crucial, for there are too many instances of their being more intent on self-satisfaction, even self-glorification, than on what they should contribute to the overall end product, namely worship. Maybe what the musicians provide in a service is satisfying to them, but it can all too easily be a lot less rewarding, and is certainly inescapable, for those on the receiving end.

A similarly less-than-ideal situation occurs when cathedral choirs are on holiday and visiting parish church choirs or other groups take over. Being in a strange and probably much larger building, with the organ maybe some distance from the singers, provides problems enough in itself, but this can be made worse when choirs elect to sing music which apes the cathedral repertoire in its complexity and which is probably beyond their realistic capabilities. If only they would confine themselves to simpler music well sung, the end product would be more edifying for the listener.

This leads us to cathedral music, sung day by day as it has been down through the centuries by highly skilled musicians for and on behalf of a smallish community, most of whom do not anyhow wish to participate audibly other than maybe in the singing of hymns. Both by its nature and intent cathedral music is not congregational music, while the concept of silent worship is not always fully understood by either clergy or laity. Many misunderstandings no doubt derive from the reasoning underlying our new liturgies and their emphasis on involvement. This, however, does not imply a free-for-all in which everyone is doing everything all the time. Worship is in many respects akin to a jig-saw puzzle in which every piece – clergy, musicians and laity – are relevant and essential components of the complete picture. Leave out one of the pieces and the picture is incomplete. One important factor is that the Church of England, unlike some other denominations, provides a flexibility in the conduct of its worship which aims to cater for all persuasions – high, low, and middle-of-the-road alike.

Endemic to all we have so far considered is the fact that music is the one art form which needs a third party – an interpreter – to bring to life a page of dots, blobs, lines and other hieroglyphics indecipherable to those who cannot read music. Compare and contrast this with painting, architecture, and the constantly changing panorama of natural beauty. These, being visual, are instantly discernable, and consequently interpreted by us as and how we see fit, without any third-party aid. Because music is an aural and mobile art it is in this respect unique. Once it is heard, only the memory of that particular performance is retained in the mind. Although we can listen to music or perform it again and again it is never exactly the same on each occasion. This in its turn places a considerable onus on those performing it and accounts for the various interpretations there are available on disc – thirty or forty of them of Beethoven's 5th Symphony alone. This is in some ways akin to how a producer elects to present a play. It also has a certain affinity with cathedral worship where the music, as I suggested earlier, provides the aural constituent while the eye concentrates on the visual in terms of architecture, glass and artefacts. The two combine in a wondrously rewarding way.

In what follows I have sought to explore in some depth not only what music can of itself do to enrich words but how important it is for church musicians to be highly perceptive of their role, with the need to tease out to the full the possibilities inherent in its interpretation so that the music never sounds perfunctory or routine. To achieve the very best and the most convincing performance, while bearing in mind the repetitive nature of much liturgical worship, this must be the prime objective of the church musicians. We shall see that the best vocal music derives from composers who understand the full significance of the words they elect to set and who draw it out so that the resultant is inspirational for the worshipper. It is as simple, and as demanding, as that. The onus on the musicians is crucial though not always perceived as such. Could this be because choir directors and their forces are not always on the right wavelength, first and foremost as participating worshippers?

For the composer, the point of departure is the existence of a rich anthology of texts – the Bible, the Book of Common Prayer, the Psalter and, of course, the wealth of poetry of all ages from the early mystics, through George Herbert, Traherne and the great hymn writers of each generation, to poets such as that profound moulder of words, T. S. Eliot. What a strange contrast emerges from many secular texts – not least opera where the plot and the use of words is so often but a fragile framework on which to hang the music. Kenneth Clark, in *Civilisation*, said that 'what is too silly to be said may be sung – well, yes; but what is too subtle to be said, or too deeply felt, or too revealing or too mysterious – these things can also be sung, and only sung'.[3]

Finally, and in surveying the entire panorama, it is interesting to reflect that so much church music is either penitential or seasonal. This is especially true of the sixteenth to nineteenth centuries, both in Britain and on the continent. Today there is much more exuberantly joyful church music, maybe because we live in an age much more conditioned than previously to rhythm, though in some ways it is akin to the complicated and complex rhythms at the heart of much medieval music. Today, William Mathias, Kenneth Leighton and John Rutter are but three 'rhythmic' composers, with the latter having at his fingertips a seemingly never-ending store of subtle rhythmic devices allied to an equally fertile vocal and harmonic constituent. After all, the sum total of melody, rhythm and harmony is basic to *all* music, whether of past centuries or newly composed for worship today.

2

Points of Departure

At the outset, stress needs to be laid on certain factors which apply across the board:

1. Vocal music is *part* of the machinery of corporate worship, its sole objective being to enrich what otherwise would be spoken. It is not the be-all and end-all.

2. It follows that only the very best in performance will suffice. Singing demands unremitting effort, not least in rehearsal. This is more relevant when compared with an instrumentalist who makes sound pure and simple, for the singer has the additional responsibility of projecting words.

3. While diction is obviously of the essence, too often we encounter slackness in this respect, with distorted vowel sounds and consonants lacking crispness and vitality. Add to this the fact that so much church music moves slowly, softly, and sometimes within a resonant building, and the need for clearly defined diction is imperative if the listener is to benefit. Common mispronunciations, especially on radio and television, such as 'terday' for 'today' and 'wust' for 'west' are bad enough when spoken but far worse when sung.

4. While the thrust of this book is directed towards the repertoire of the Anglican Church, its comments and conclu-

sions are applicable across the denominational board from cathedrals and parish churches to Free Church chapels. A major objective is to help humble organists who wish to improve their skills so that the worshipper receives, as Francis Jackson, sometime organist of York Minster, suggests, 'an experience which will live on in the memory when the merely exciting and ephemeral performance is forgotten'.

5. The examples quoted are by no means exhaustive though they illustrate points made. Even if some of them are from works which not every choir will sing, the principles and the suggestions made are applicable to all concerned.

6. We live in an age where authenticity is very much the order of the day, and scholarship and the fashions of each period of musical history are increasingly being brought to bear by specialist choirs. These principles cannot realistically be practised if the forces and techniques are not available. There is always the additional danger of church music being prone to a measure of eccentricity, and nowhere more than in the chanting of psalms, as we shall later see.

7. The final word must be to emphasize the need for the pursuit of excellence. This is as basic to music as to any art form whether aural or visual. Interpretation is therefore very much to the fore in what now follows.

3

Hymns

We shall see that when the faith has been sung it has spread. An outburst of singing is associated with every advance the Church has made: indeed without hymns there has been no forward movement.

Bertram L. Barnby, *In Concert Sing*

Introduction

Hymnody is probably the most important, and certainly the most significant, aspect of church music. Of all the types of music used in worship, hymns stand out as the one inescapable constituent in that whatever the form of service, every few minutes worship will in most instances be punctuated by hymnody, with clergy, choir, organist and, not least, congregation brought together in joint involvement. People love to sing hymns and a hymn can become an act of worship in itself and often be more memorable than the spoken parts of a service.

A hymn stands or falls by its tune which in some instances is superior to the words. Cyril Taylor, himself no mean hymn scholar and the composer of ABBOT'S LEIGH, one of the great hymn tunes of our time, always maintained that it is invariably the tune, and not the words, that provides the long-term memorability – and the nostalgia. It is the tune, especially when it is indissolubly linked with its associated words, which brings a hymn to life and gives the truest expression to the words – a further example of speech being beautified.

All this, and more, lays great responsibility on the musicians who too often sideline, or even offload, hymns as irrelevant and perfunctory nuisances to be perforce endured, and dispensed with, as speedily as possible to make way for choice titbits such as anthems and choir settings of the liturgy. This unimaginative approach can influence a congregation who will then probably play their part in an equally uninterested, or at best routine, way. If the hymn tune is itself in equal value notes with little, if any, rhythmic variation, it can all too easily result in dull sounds, for it is all too easy for hymns to be indifferently churned out verse by verse. What opportunities are then missed. Add to this the chances of well-known hymns being sung far too frequently and you have a further disincentive. All this shows that the responsibilities of the musicians cannot be over-emphasized. By marked contrast, when hymns are played and sung with conviction and with an awareness of the mood and character of each, this quickly rubs off on the congregation who in their turn are then more likely to appreciate the choir's anthems.

In the Church of England the choice, rehearsal and overall preparation of hymns is too seldom given the emphasis and priority that should be afforded them, especially in those instances where hymnody is *the* musical constituent of a service. You need go no further than some of our cathedrals to see the way in which choirs switch off during the singing of hymns – as for that matter in the said parts of the services. Worship is a joint and all-embracing preoccupation for all concerned, though this does not necessarily imply, even in contemporary liturgies, everyone doing everything *all the time* as some of the clergy insist.

A glance at the index of authors in any hymn book will reveal not only the breadth and variety of the poetry on offer but, more to the point, how wide-ranging hymns are as the work of a multitude of authors of different persuasions and denominations down through the centuries. All of this is in marked contrast to the contemporary doggerel, often trivial in the extreme, which is now in such wide use. The charasmatic appeal of these songs is no excuse for the theological deficiencies of many of their words.

As in all vocal music, the words, not the music, must always be the determining point of departure. Texts need to be scrutinized as much by those who choose hymns as by those responsible for leading music in worship. This, incidentally, applies particularly to the need for familiar hymns at services, such as funerals, where non-churchgoers are present. Too often we fall short in these respects, not least through our lack of vision in the dilatory way in which we sing and play hymns. We are also reluctant to explore the possibilities of good alternative tunes, particularly when a long established tune would seem to be unremittingly locked into certain words. In practice, the use of a different tune as an alternative – though not necessarily a substitute – can throw an entirely new light on a text, as I will later show. Even so, it would be a brave soul who would contemplate substituting a new tune for 'Abide with me' or 'Rock of ages'!

Some Examples

To illustrate the points so far made, we need to consider some more or less traditionally moulded texts and see what the music does, or fails to do, in taking the words that stage further.

Firmly I believe and truly. These words of great strength and conviction are enhanced in no uncertain way when married to William Boyce's tune HALTON HOLGATE. In every line of every verse the word stresses gain through the rise and fall of the melodic contours, even in the last line when the tune falls to its lowest notes, yet loses nothing in the process. As in so many good hymns the initial line sets the mood for what is to come. This hymn needs to be sung with a full-bodied legato, while allowing lightness to the stepwise movement of the quavers in the third line. In verse 3 the punctuation needs to be clearly marked: 'supremely – solely' and 'him the holy – him the strong'. The final verse is a superb doxology and can gain from being sung in a broad unison, though the need, or use, of free harmonies in the accompaniment is questionable. What is there can hardly be bettered.

By marked contrast, the tune SHIPSTON, which has always been used in *The English Hymnal*, though nice enough, is a jaunty folk tune and comes off second best, nowhere doing for the words what HALTON HOLGATE does. Worse still, and by far, is Patrick Appleford's jerky, insignificant and insensitive tune ALTON, a typical example of what the Twentieth Century Church Light Music Group were adept at producing.

Through the night of doubt and sorrow. In retrospect it seems strange that Dykes' ST OSWALD has held sway for so long. Its weak first line with altos and basses permanently on the note D may be in small part made up for by the third and fourth lines, but it needed the vision of Martin Shaw to grasp in the 1930s the underlying theme of movement – 'marching', 'stepping', and 'treading' – before we reach the 'far eternal shore'.

MARCHING is a superb tune which needs to be sung and played in a way that not only mirrors movement as the basis of the text but continues to build up melodically to the high notes which neatly partner to such good effect the climax in the fourth line of each verse.

Hymns Ancient and Modern goes a stage further by including Parry's RUSTINGTON. While the four-line verses work well enough with MARCHING, Parry's eight-line tune gives an added breadth to the text with the words set out in this way. The two modulations are simple yet add that something, especially in the second half where the highest notes come in the fourth quarter, a bonus feature of so many of the best hymn tunes and Anglican chants. The music needs to be sung with a well sustained and generous legato, and certainly broader than the quick-step of MARCHING. While there is much to be said for both these tunes, each of which throws a different complexion on the words, I would on balance put my money on RUSTINGTON, though certainly in no detriment to Martin Shaw. Ringing the changes is no bad thing so as to experience the impact each tune has in its own way. It is strange that with these two splendid tunes in circulation, there is still a considerable regard for ST OSWALD. Perhaps it is an example of 'We know what we like, and we like what we know'.

The spacious firmament on high has one familiar tune, and one only, but how superb it is. Whoever the eighteenth-century J. Sheeles was, he could certainly write a good tune and one which fits Addison's great hymn of creation like the proverbial glove, the more so if you use the *New English Hymnal* harmonization which is stronger and more telling than *A & M*. A stroke of near genius here is the repetition of the final line of the words in each verse. This is even more effective in the last verse with its superb summing-up. Every singer and organist should be required to read the words again and again as pure poetry before singing them. It follows that the musicians need to have something in reserve to highlight the repeated final line. While the pause marks in the *NEH* version are best dispensed with in the interests of continuity and flow, there is much to be said for a broadening out in the final line of all, with a short pause on the word 'voice' in the sixth line of the last verse – though it would be wise to warn the congregation in advance. A similar example was used to great effect in York Minster when Sir Edward Bairstow was organist and where, in the third verse of 'Jesus Christ is risen today', there was a great crescendo and broadening out at 'Now above the sky he's King' with full organ, plus tuba. The effect in that great resonant building was electrifying and you really knew that Easter had come. The effectiveness of devices such as this derive to a great extent from their rarity value.

Lead, kindly Light. Here is an example of a much-loved tune that does nothing for the words, the very reverse in fact. Dykes' LUX BENIGNA is for ever stopping and starting and so destroys the underlying theme of movement in the words with their repeated emphasis on 'lead thou me on'.

By marked contrast, ALBERTA, inspired by Sir William Harris's travels through the Canadian Rockies, does everything to enhance the words. Its broad unison and momentum, together with the melodic climax in the last line, produces a memorable effect.

Let all the world in every corner sing. The hymn poetry of the metaphysical writer George Herbert stands head and shoulders above much else, and with good reason. This particular example effervesces from beginning to end with such an enthusiastic outpouring of praise. He does it all in sixteen lines, two of which appear four times. Harwood's LUCKINGTON, and no other tune, is firmly wedded to this great paean of praise. He gets the emphasis just right by mirroring word climaxes, through either high notes or notes of longer length. As a result, here is a fine example of words and music going hand in hand, the one enhancing the other. Musicians need to spell out and emphasize the important moments in the broad phrases, such as the use twice in the second verse of an emphatic 'must', while holding something in reserve for the final 'my God and King' in each verse.

Teach me, my God and King, another Herbert hymn, is very different in both concept and the use of words. As Bertram Barnby points out, 'of the 118 words in the five verses we sing today, 105 are monosyllables'.[1] This calls for perception, for while the tune SANDYS is not particularly memorable it does help if all concerned view each verse as a four-line entity and project it as such, while allowing due space for those many monosyllables, if the hymn is not to become chatty. The text is too good for this to happen.

How shall I sing that majesty. These superb words by the seventeenth-century writer John Mason have until recently been associated with either SOLL'S SEIN or Vaughan Williams' THIRD MODE MELODY, neither of which does much for the breadth of the text.

Vaughan Williams' arrangement of the English traditional melody KINGSFOLD is a happier marriage though the real breakthrough has only emerged in recent years with Ken Naylor's superb COE FEN, now firmly established as one of the great tunes of the twentieth century. It does everything a hymn tune ideally should do in terms of melody and harmony, and with an unerring sense of climax where needed – and expected. Although the words in themselves are demanding, how transformed they become when linked with this fine music. To experience this hymn and this tune for the first time is a revelation, the more so in the summing-up of the second half of the last verse. It would be a frigid person not to be moved by the poetic insight of this hymn, let alone the music which is on a par with another fine contemporary tune, Cyril Taylor's ABBOT'S LEIGH, which possesses all the qualities which single out a successful hymn tune. Its melodic structure, so eminently singable, includes two upward leaps of an octave which work because they move from a weak to a strong beat. The composer regularly bemoaned congregations singing F#

instead of D three notes before the end. Although F# seems
more logical this is not what Cyril Taylor wrote. The matching harmonic strength, not least in the sudden shift (not
modulation) at the half-way mark which then takes us briefly
to B minor before returning to the home key, is equally
remarkable. As with COE FEN, the music makes the hymn
memorable.

Christ triumphant, ever reigning is a further example of a
contemporary winner, and for all the same reasons. Michael
Saward's words have been admirably captured, and enhanced, through John Barnard's fine tune GUITING POWER.
It is the rise and fall of the melodic line, its ready singability,
and the harmonic grip, together with the brief modulations in
the second half, which combine to produce what hymnody at
its best is all about.

Praise to the holiest in the height. Dykes falls short with his
tune GERONTIUS, popular though it may be. While this
matches the words in the first and last verses, with the music
moving upwards to 'in the height' and downwards for 'and
in the depth be praise', this does not work for the remaining
verses, all of which commence on an unimportant word
musically accommodated by a high note sung on the first
beat of the bar. Choirs need to be sensitive to this if the full
impact and meaning of Cardinal Newman's fine words are to
be carried forward through the music. In all instances there
needs to be an instinctive feeling of onward movement in the
phrase shapes:

A <u>sec</u> – ond <u>Ad</u> – am to the <u>fight</u>

Nevertheless it would be hard to dislodge the popularity of
this tune despite its defects. Terry's BILLING avoids the
problems in the second, third and fourth lines, where the

upbeat in the music takes account of each line in the text commencing with an unimportant word.

Somervell's CHORUS ANGELORUM deals more successfully with lines three and four than with the first two lines. In all instances here there are subtle points which need sensitive care if the full potential of the words is to be realized.

The Church of God a kingdom is is another instance where *EH* got it wrong, CAPEL doing little or nothing for a text of considerable strength.

This jaunty traditional tune is similarly partnered by *A. & M.* using UNIVERSITY, a chatty tune and good enough in its way, but not for these words. CREDITON, effectively used for a hymn for the Transfiguration in the New Standard Edition of *A. & M.*, leaves one in little doubt as to what the Church of God is all about, not least in the last verse with its sting in the tail. There is a similar instance in the final verse of 'Jesus, where'er thy people meet'.

Love divine, all loves excelling. Here is a yet further example of a fine hymn text not well served by a popular tune, Stainer's being a trite utterance with chromatic overtones adding to its sugary character.

Couple these words to BLAENWERN or ABBOT'S LEIGH and you immediately have a very different concept. Both tunes are for eight-line hymns and by treating Charles Wesley's text in this way the overall strength is apparent, particularly at the end. But the Stainer tune is very popular and will not easily be dislodged, though by ringing the changes it is soon apparent which tunes do something positive for the words.

Holy, holy, holy. This text by Heber majestically portrays so much and in a pictorial way, with its reference to the first verse of Psalm 63 in the second line, and later to the Song of

Hannah in the Book of Samuel. Bertram Barnby suggests that 'no other hymn so majestically comprehends God's attributes'.[2] Dykes' NICAEA is a wellnigh perfect musical partner, not least in repeating the music for the thrice-holy in lines one and three of the first and last verses, but overall even more by its melodic and harmonic integrity. This does much for the words if sung steadily and with breadth, especially at 'Ho – ly, ho – ly, ho – ly' where the commas will be the better emphasized by lightening the second syllable and by a definite crescendo through to the third 'holy'.

There is something to be said in favour of sometimes linking a tune associated with a particular hymn to other words. This can give an entirely new dimension to both words and music, though this is suggested more as an alternative than a substitute.

When I survey the wondrous cross. ROCKINGHAM is all but indissolubly linked with Watts' words, and with very good reason, for it so admirably matches their beauty, not least in the last verse ('Were the whole realm of nature mine . . .'), surely one of the most profound and demanding verses in all hymnody. Nevertheless, there are a number of false accents, such as that on 'all the vain things', which is not helped by a two-beat note on 'in', and on a high note, in the previous line. Worse still is 'sor-row and love'.

While it would be unthinkable to attempt to displace ROCKINGHAM, the folksong WALY, WALY, which is set to 'An upper room did our Lord prepare' in *A. & M.* (NSE), is a very acceptable alternative, providing an entirely new, but no less valid, complexion to the words.

The Church's one foundation is firmly linked to S. S. Wesley's AURELIA, one of his less successful tunes, certainly in the first and last two lines. It fails to match up to the robustness of the words and as such is an example of music detracting from the words. This is not altogether surprising as Wesley originally wrote the tune for 'Jerusalem the golden'.

KING'S LYNN, Vaughan Williams' effective arrangement of a folk melody, is a far happier liaison, though, as an experiment, be bold and try singing these words to ST. THEODULPH, the tune used for 'All glory, laud, and honour'. You will experience how an entirely new dimension is revealed in the words, with an added sting in the tail by having to repeat the first four lines of the opening to make the music fit the text. Then revert to AURELIA and see the difference. The problem here is that for many congregations Wesley's tune is much loved and, although it is by contrast a fairly static and dull tune very much lacking in vision, it would nevertheless be hard to dislodge.

Eternal Ruler of the ceaseless round. A further example in this context is the tune YORKSHIRE, usually sung once a year to 'Christians, awake! salute the happy morn' – not the best of Christmas hymns as it is so lengthy and ponderous in unfolding its story. In choosing a tune for 'Eternal Ruler of the ceaseless round', fine though Gibbons' SONG 1 is, YORKSHIRE will throw a new complexion on the words, but again is suggested only as an alternative. It is included in *Common Praise*, the new hymn book which has succeeded *Hymns Ancient and Modern*.

Some General Observations

Dynamics

Many of the most successful hymns relay their message by telling a story, and a teaching one at that. Others rehearse the stages of our Lord's life. Patrick Appleford's 'Jesus, humble was your birth' makes its point in the third line of each verse, urging us 'every day in all we do' to follow our Lord's example, the repetition providing a unifying element to good effect. 'Jesus, good above all other' is a similar example as is 'We have a gospel to proclaim'. I would not for one moment suggest that musicians mirror these different events through an overlarded sentimental approach such as the once popular dramatic contrasts in the final verse of 'Abide with me', where 'in life' was sung loudly and 'in death' pianissimo. In Victorian times death was invariably spoken of in hushed tones whereas we surely do not ask 'O Lord, abide with me' only in life, but even more so in death and the looking forward to its fulfilment in eternal life. A careful assessing of how logical dynamics can emphasize certain points will add to the completeness of a hymn; the musicians – and congregations – must not only sense these but be able to relay them to good effect.

Some hymns are effective in summing up their message with a sting in the tail, such as Sydney's Carter's 'The Lord of the Dance' where he forcibly, and maybe embarrassingly, says 'I'll live in you if you'll live in me'. Mention was made earlier of the final verse of 'When I survey the wondrous Cross', which is one of the most demanding statements for any of us to take on board, as in another way is the last verse of 'O thou who camest from above'.

As alluded to earlier, it is all too easy for choirs to sing, as for organists to play, each and every hymn in the same way, which sometimes means a dull monotony until the last verse which is invariably loud, and with a sizeable rallentando at the end. Hymns can take on an entirely different complexion and meaning when the final verse is given a quiet and reflective treatment. Similarly, there are occasions which demand a different approach. The great festivals with their large numbers and sense of excitement call for a robustness as compared with a quiet Lenten or evening service, with perhaps a mere handful in the congregation.

It is quite extraordinary how insensitive musicians can be towards hymnody. In this they not only miss out on much that is relevant to public worship but additionally they do a disservice to the congregations they serve. Hymns, by and large, are, as with congregational settings of the Eucharist, the one and only aspect of church music in which the people in the pews rely on the musicians to lead them. This can be an inspiring exercise, though I well remember a television 'Songs of Praise' where virtually everything was done in the wrong way. 'Forth in thy name, O Lord, I go' is a superb poem of dedication popularly linked with Orlando Gibbons' SONG 34. On this occasion the conductor relentlessly thrashed the subtle rhythms in so rigid a way as to distort the shape of the music. This, and the unnecessary extravagance of his conducting, did nothing to enrich the words, and this was reflected in the way the people sang. The music here demands a quietly reflective, but positive, interpretation.

Choice of Tune

Leading on from this, how crucial it is to marry the right tune to the words. There is little excuse nowadays for not doing so as most of the recent hymn books often suggest alternative tunes. Some are more readily interchangeable than others. Two Long Metre tunes are random cases in point. NIAGARA, with its catchy rhythm, needs to be better known, as does WARRINGTON. Another winner calling for better exposure is 'New songs of celebration render', fine words of Erik Routley based on Psalm 98 and set to RENDEZ À DIEU, a robust sixteenth-century tune with a splendid rhythmic basis, particularly in the fifth line.

Rhythm

A number of tunes written as four crotchets in a bar are much more effective when taken as two minims. This produces greater breadth. A good example is HIGHWOOD which greatly benefits from such treatment and avoids any possible fussiness, particularly in the words. It is also interesting to see how many hymn tunes are in triple time, though with the need to avoid any semblance of a waltz. ST CLEMENT ('The day thou gavest, Lord, is ended') is a particularly good example of this. A further danger can arise from tunes where repetition plays a major part. ST DENIO, in itself a not altogether distinguished tune, has three of its four lines musically identical. LLANFAIR ('Hail the day that sees him rise') does exactly the same. But there are some fine and eminently singable Welsh tunes, not least HYFRYDOL and BLAENWERN, both of which are extensively used, and with good reason.

In the final count the test with every tune is whether melodically and harmonically it will bear necessary repetition or whether it will pall with use.

Refrains

In each of the six verses of 'Thy hand, O God, has guided' the final line sums up what has gone before with 'one Church, one faith, one Lord'. In terms of singing there must be a real sense of climax with the punctuation clearly marking 'Church – faith – Lord'. Although the hymn from start to finish is a great surge of positive statements, all concerned need to keep something in reserve for the refrain, not least in holding on to the final note for a full five beats as indicated, with a clearly marked final consonant coming at the *start* of the sixth beat. A steady dynamic build-up will add to the emphasis.

'O come, all ye faithful' is cast in a similar mould though

with 'O come, let us adore him' sung three times in succession. This should be cumulative and not a mere repetition. The key word is 'come' which will be strengthened if singers think of 'k' rather than 'c', as in the German *komm*.

In 'Lo, he comes with clouds descending' the fifth line of the first and last verses is a three-fold 'Alleluia', an oft-repeated word in hymnody which will gain in impact through a dynamic thrust suggesting onward movement. In the Easter hymn 'Alleluia, Alleluia, hearts to heaven and voices raise' the vitality of the word is helped by the tune LUX EOI:

'A   -   lay - loo   -   ya'

And, incidentally, the word is *not*, as we frequently hear it pronounced, 'Allelulia'.

'All hail the power of Jesus' name' has, in MILES LANE, music which caters admirably for a four-fold repetition of 'crown him', with 'the crownéd Lord of all' the final statement. Articulating 'crown' as 'ker-roun' will heighten the grip of the word. Double consonants always need to be clearly articulated. If the hymn is sung too slowly at the outset the long notes of the refrain can diminish the impetus, so a fairly brisk tempo is needed. There is a stress fault at the start of verse five where, because of the musical accent and the upward movement of the tune, we usually sing 'Sin-NERRS'. (A similarly misplaced accent can easily occur at the start of the final verse of CRIMOND – 'good-NESS'). Ferguson's LADYWELL is a commendable alternative tune which sets out the words in eight-line verses to good effect, not least in its treatment of the refrain. Another effective instance is 'Lift high the Cross' though here the singing of all twelve verses plus twelve refrains can become something of a marathon.

Gaps between Verses

These are important in providing the spaces needed between verses, as in the reading of poetry. Perhaps even more to the point is the physical need for singers to have time to take a breath, something some organists seem unaware of. These spaces must not be too short or too long, but rather dictated by a continuity in rhythm. They must also be consistent between each verse of a hymn, though sometimes the final note of a tune as written seems inordinately long. In FRANCONIA, for example, the final note is in practice usually given two beats, with two beats' rest before the next verse. By adopting similar principles towards all hymnody the start of verses will be more unanimous and will avoid the untidiness which can be experienced. An exception to this is 'Bright the vision that delighted' where ideally verses 3 and 6 should be linked without a break with what precedes them, though if this practice is adopted congregations will need to be warned. In *A. & M.* there is an effective descant which highlights to good effect verses 3 and 6. The three-fold 'holy' needs some degree of punctuation and will be best achieved by merely stressing the first syllable and lightening the second – 'HO – li' (not 'ho – LEE').

Amens

These are generally out of fashion nowadays though a doxology should always have one. If Amens are to be sung they should be a strong and positive 'So be it', with dynamics kept up. At all costs avoid the sentimental slow lingering death accentuated by a sizeable rallentando and diminuendo.

Free Harmonies

While some of the published examples are imaginative and can add much to the completeness of a hymn, they need to be used sparingly and not necessarily confined to a last verse. Some organists prefer to make them up on the spur of the moment and can, as a result, come to grief *en route*. Relatively few organists have the skill to produce convincing – and inspiring – off-the-cuff harmonies. In the wrong hands these can do a disservice and be an embarrassment to all concerned, if maybe not to the satisfied perpetrator. The moral should be only to embark on this if you can with impunity better what the composer wrote. As a prime example of how well this can be done, you need look no further than the David Willcocks' free harmonizations in *Carols for Choirs* or those by Bairstow published by Oxford University Press. Those by Willcocks are probably the more effective in that they only come up once or twice a year and therefore have something of a novelty, and rarity, value.

The Organ Introduction

The two reasons for this are to remind people of the tune and to set its tempo. It is therefore counter-productive when an organist concludes the play-over with a sizeable rallentando which destroys the object of the exercise. Two lines of introduction are adequate, not an entire verse as in the United States. Even less helpful is the growing custom of playing the final bars of a tune. It is surely the opening by which we readily recognize a tune, not its ending. The choice of stops should relay the mood of the hymn. It is as unhelpful to play over 'Jesus Christ is risen today' on flutes as it is to introduce 'Abide with me' on full organ. Legato for quiet meditative hymns needs to be contrasted with a more decisive approach for robust hymns using a detached right hand while left hand

and pedals are legato. Every hymn has its own speed determined by its style and mood, the acoustics of a church and the number of people singing.

Choice of Hymns

Although this does not perhaps strictly come within the remit of this book, it nevertheless has some bearing. The need for the right hymn at the right juncture of every service should at least be appreciated by musicians though the choice will not necessarily be their responsibility. While Morning and Evening Prayer and special services are relatively easy and flexible, the constraints of the Eucharist, especially if this happens to be a Parish Communion, calls for careful consideration. The guidelines readily provided today in most hymn books and elsewhere are invaluable reference points, particularly where modern liturgies are involved.

There are four main slots – Introit, Gradual, Offertory and Post-Communion – where hymnody usually has to be accommodated. These are crucial junctures where considerable thought needs to be exercised as to the right choice.

At the start of the service something of an invitatory nature, and fairly short unless there is a sizeable procession of clergy and choir, is needed to set the scene. While 'Come, let us join our cheerful songs' and 'Father, hear the prayer we offer' spring to mind as suitable choices, there are plenty of others, not least for festival occasions. The onus here on the musicians is considerable and much will depend on how they approach this opening hymn as to whether the service subsequently takes off or not.

For the Gradual, all that is needed is something short and reflective, such as 'O Holy Spirit, Lord of grace', 'Blest are the pure in heart' or 'Rise and hear! The Lord is speaking'.

At the Offertory a substantial hymn is needed during the

preparation of the elements and the taking up of the Offertory. 'Alleluia, sing to Jesus' never fails at this juncture, though 'Lord, enthroned in heavenly splendour' is often over-used.

The final hymn, which should *always* come before the Blessing and the Dismissal, should send us out into the world as a musical complement to the prayer we shall have said if we are using the ASB or *Common Worship*. The hymn here needs to be robust in sending us on our way without undue delay, and not, as I once experienced, all twelve verses of 'Lift high the Cross'. We need to be aware of pitfalls which can happen through choosing a hymn because of the first verse, such as 'Praise to the Lord, the Almighty, the King of creation' which seems on the face of it to be highly suitable until the fourth line – 'now to his temple draw near' – just as we are leaving church. This is a far more suitable hymn as an Introit.

In some churches a hymn, or hymns, find a place during the communion of the people. As the congregation are at this time more occupied with getting to and from the communion rail than with singing, this can be an ideal opportunity for the choir to sing something on their own, perhaps an un-familiar communion hymn or a motet. Alternatively, a quiet piece of organ music is suitable – or even silence.

A further consideration on the choice of hymns arises when a preacher wants a certain hymn as an illustration to the sermon.

Plainsong Hymns

As the Church's folk music these can be traced back to the very earliest days, though today they are a somewhat rare-fied, and specialized, aspect of hymnody. Being cast in free rhythm they are not all that easy for congregations weaned on tunes in a measured rhythmic pulse, and moving generally note by note and word by word; plainsong may well have a whole cluster of notes to one word, or even one syllable. Apart from one or two hardy favourites such as 'Come, Holy Ghost' (VENI, CREATOR SPIRITUS), 'Before the ending of the day' in the service of Compline, and to a lesser degree the Passiontide hymn 'The royal banners forward go', this being a fairly florid example, we are seldom expected to sing plainsong hymns. Being purely melodic, plainsong is best sung unaccompanied for the most satisfying and authentic performance. It needs moreover to be sung lightly, almost in a half voice, and should move at the speed of the spoken word while taking into account that when two or more notes are allotted to one word or syllable, the first note should be slightly emphasized and the remaining notes sung lightly. All in all, the subtleties of plainsong are considerable and rule out effective congregational participation. As there are now so many CDs of plainsong available, and so well sung, these can be something of a blueprint for choirs to emulate even though plainsong is still to a degree confined to the monastic environment.

Congregational Choir Practices

While for various reasons there are now all but consigned to history, there are valid and probably better alternative options. Some of the newer tunes are instant winners, being so well conceived in melody and harmony, and are thus not priorities for rehearsal. Others need some introduction to congregations. At Salisbury Cathedral when a new and unfamiliar hymn is to be sung, the Precentor briefly speaks about it before the service commences, pointing out what is needed and any pitfalls likely to be encountered. The organist then plays the tune, the Precentor sings a verse, and then the congregation. By doing this the people are more likely at least to give the new tune a hearing than if it were thrust on them without any prior warning. This is a simple psychological expedient.

Summing Up

Because of the importance of hymnody in public worship, certain considerations as to the way in which they are sung, played and, not least, chosen, need to be emphasized, and I make no excuse for underlining some of the things said earlier.

1. As there is so much good traditionally moulded material to draw on there is no excuse for a narrow or safe choice, nor for the frequent repetition of certain hymns which may be favourites of the vicar. It is, however, important to ensure that familiar hymns are in the main used at services such as weddings and funerals where non-churchgoers, even non-Christians, are present.

2. One cannot highlight too forcibly the apparent lack of interest shown by many musicians towards hymnody. This can so easily result in any lead they should give to a congregation being handicapped by the dull and monotonous way which underlines so much of the singing and playing of hymns in church and cathedral alike. The fact that many hymn tunes are more or less a succession of notes of equal values does not help matters. This encourages every word and syllable to be given the same emphasis, or thump, such as

    Rejoice ! the Lord is King

instead of

    Re – joice ! (comma) the Lord is King

The absence of phrasing in both singing and playing inevitably results in distorting the natural flow of the words, and often their sense, as for example in the Easter hymn 'Jesus lives!' Here, if the third note is made a crotchet followed by a quaver rest, the two exclamatory words which preface and highlight each verse make sense, a simple expedient which makes all the difference to the entire concept. The onus on the musicians is to make the words come alive through an intelligent and meaningful approach as in speaking. How often we hear at the end of each verse of 'Thy hand, O God, has guided' a string of words equally stressed, and unpunctuated, instead of 'One <u>Church</u> – one <u>faith</u> – one <u>Lord</u>'.

3. Double consonants demand clear and precise articulation. Compare the vitality of 'ger-rate' with the dullness of a hurried 'gwate' – this is but one of the countless examples.

4. It follows that the meaning and message of each line of every hymn needs to be relayed with conviction. When two lines run on without a break:

'Thou our life! O let us be
Rooted, grafted, built on thee.'

the two beats on the unimportant word 'be' need a strengthening of tone to carry the word sense over to the next line. This is the point of climax to which the earlier part of the text builds up:

<u>root</u> – ed, 'graf – ted, <u>built</u> on <u>thee</u>'.

It should be sung with regard not only for the commas but for the build-up to the climax on the final word 'thee'.

5. We have additionally to take into account the fact that by no means all hymn texts are readily sustainable, even

reliable, in terms of theology and doctrine, as in the hymn
by Canon Crum (one of the original proprietors of *Hymns
A & M*) which states

> In meadow and field the cattle are good
> And the rabbits are thinking no evil.
> The anemones bright are refined and polite
> And all the primroses are civil.
>
> O once in a while we obey with a smile
> And are ever so modest and prudent;
> But it's not very long before something is wrong
> And somebody's done what he shouldn't.

Richard Watson, in *The English Hymn* (Oxford University
Press, 1997) sums up much of what this chapter is about
when he writes:

> The loss of hymns from school assemblies, and the
> almost exclusive use of modern hymns or songs in some
> churches, suggest that the older generations now living
> may well be the last for whom the traditional hymn is an
> integral part of their emotional and spiritual culture.
> The English hymn is in danger of becoming a subject for
> academic study rather than a living form of worship,
> and I wanted to write this book while it was still alive,
> while it was still some kind of presence in liturgy and
> life.[3]

4

Psalms

Introduction

Here we have a somewhat different ball game, a fundamental constraint being that, unlike hymns with their mainly consistent metre and rhyme, no two psalm verses are of the same length in terms of the number of words. The freedom this engenders, as compared with the discipline inherent to the construction of hymns, brings with it a number of varying problems. Although the speech rhythm method of singing psalms (of which more later) is today the widely accepted approach, identical principles apply to their performance as to all other vocal music. Whereas whatever hymn book we elect to use there is a basic consistency in the poetry, with the psalms we have to take account not only of the various methods of pointing used to accommodate the music to the words but also the various translations on offer today. Whereas there is one, and one only hymn 'Abide with me', the psalms can provide a confusing situation.

Furthermore, while singing the psalms to Anglican chants remains the most familiar method to Anglicans, if not nowadays the most widely used, it brings with it considerable constraints stemming from the need for a group of people to sing together tidily while using free-style speech rhythm. Even in cathedrals where the psalms are sung every day, considerable rehearsal is needed. Despite these problems it is interesting to see other denominations using the psalms – and to Anglican pointing – in their services, with such books as the Methodist *Hymns and Psalms*.

Prior to the Oxford Movement in the last century, the singing of psalms in the Church of England was confined to metrical versions, many of which continue to be widely used even if we are not always aware of it. These include 'All people that on earth do dwell' (Psalm 100), 'Praise the Lord! ye heavens, adore him' (Psalm 148), and 'God of mercy, God of grace' (Psalm 67). A glance through any hymn book will reveal just how many hymn texts are in fact metrical versions of the psalms, thus emphasizing how much easier it is for congregations to sing psalms in this way. In some instances, particularly Scottish metrical psalms, texts can leave much to be desired in their sheer banality and forced attempts to produce rhyme. It has to be said, though, that some of the now discarded verses of familiar hymns are little better, such as this verse in 'Hark, the glad sound':

> He comes from the thick films of vice
> To purge the mental ray,
> And on the eyeballs of the blind
> To pour celestial day.

This is but one example among a number quoted in Ian Bradley's *The Penguin Book of Hymns*.

But, to revert to psalmody, at the end of the nineteenth century two pioneer psalters appeared, *The Cathedral Psalter* and *The New Cathedral Psalter*, though in both the chant took priority in a misguided attempt to make the words fit the music. This resulted in forbidding-looking examples such as:

Full
f

THE Lord is King * and hath put on **glori**-| ous ap-| parel :
　the Lord hath put on his **apparel** and | girded · him- |
　self with | strength.
2 He hath **made the round** | world so | sure : **that** it |
　cannot | be | mov-ed.

(Psalm 93 verses 1 and 2)

In the early years of the twentieth century Robert Bridges, then Poet Laureate, sought to redress the existing failings by emphasizing that the words are the prime point of departure to which the music must be fitted if the text is to be beautified. This led on to a profusion of psalters including *The St Paul's Psalter*, *The Oxford Psalter* and *The Worcester Psalter*. *The English Psalter*, the work of Sir Edward Bairstow published in 1925, was somewhat gimmicky and in the event strangely ineffective for someone so visionary and original. No two choir directors will ever agree on methods of psalm pointing and invariably will alter what they disagree with. When Sir Sydney Nicholson produced his *Parish Psalter*, it is said that Boris Ord, the organist of King's College Chapel, Cambridge, introduced it because it was the only psalter he knew of with enough space in the margins for him to make all the alterations he wanted!

All of these psalters set out to show that the natural inflexions of speech should determine the flow of the words to which is then added the music, to wit, the Anglican chant. A complication has arisen in recent years in the modernizing of the traditional prose of Coverdale as found in The Book of Common Prayer. This has resulted in *The Revised Psalter*, that used in the ASB, and a new one in the offing for *Common Worship* to be published in late 2000. As with their predecessors, these were devised to accommodate the Anglican chant. We shall later consider deviations from this method.

It must be conceded that the singing of psalms to Anglican chants is not generally a congregational pursuit, because of the inherent difficulties which free rhythm presents to a group, the more so when congregations are expected to sing from unpointed prayer books. Even experienced choirs have to exert disciplined care and control over togetherness, yet with flexibility, though it is easier when small groups are involved. This is one of the reasons why cathedral choirs excel in their daily singing of the psalms which in its turn derives from long experience over many years. In some ways the small-scale SATB choir can be likened to a string quartet where each part listens as much to the other three as to itself, not only musically but in thinking of, and interpreting, the words. It follows that a good choir can make any psalter sound convincing when sung intelligently, as can a bad choir ruin the finest psalter.

Despite all the many advances made in speech rhythm, choir directors still elect to alter the printed version when they feel they can better it.

The Words

For a full understanding when singing the psalms it is helpful to know something about the Hebrew poetry in which they are cast, which is very different from the poetry we are familiar with. A major feature is the underlying division of each verse into two distinct halves separated by a colon. This parallelism is the key to Hebrew poetry and is seen in various ways:

(1) when the two halves of a verse are complementary to each other and make an entity (37:1 and 105:1);
(2) when the two halves are specifically linked by 'and' (57:1 and 77:12);
(3) when the second half of a verse says the opposite to the first half, usually prefaced by 'but' (34:10 and 46:6).

Some of these changes of mood are to be seen in complete psalms such as 6:8 and 90:13. Other psalms are cast in ternary (ABA) form, 27 being one where verses 8–14 provide a contrasted reflective middle section. In these latter instances a change of chant is called for and is particularly effective when a more meditative section is sung to a chant in a minor key.

Many of us would gladly concede that the translation of Coverdale, as found in The Book of Common Prayer, is the happiest approach, for it is couched in such elegant language, even if his use of guesswork sometimes leaves his meaning unclear. But these are small matters when considering the psalms as a whole. Much of the allure lies in his use of words which are particularly singable and which help us to sense more readily the correct stressing. In words of two syllables we have 'godly' and 'wisdom', in those of three syllables 'inherit', 'salvation' and 'temptation', even some of four syllables which are such a delight for singers – 'indignation' and adversaries', even at least one of five syllables – 'a-bom-in-a-ble' which intrigues small choristers when 'a bomb in a bull' is suggested as a way to get this word across. (In the hymn 'O thou who camest from above' we even have a six-syllable word, 'inextinguishable'.)

The changes of mood within the course of some psalms, as mentioned earlier, call for a parallel change in the chant. If a section is rounded off with a *slight* rallentando, followed by a short gap, the following section, and its tempo, will be the more meaningful for the listener. The more ebullient verses need to move more swiftly than penitential ones. Psalm 37 is an especial example with its long and moving portrayal of the psalmist's reflections on the unrighteous which is summed up in the promise of the final two verses – another example as in some hymnody of a sting in the tail. This comes too late for a change of chant though a slight urgency and certainly a stronger dynamic will provide the necessary contrast.

Psalms 42 and 43, originally one psalm, are interspersed on three occasions with a question and answer refrain which binds together the narrative: although we may be despondent, trust in God will provide a solution, and the more so if we give him thanks. More extended, and unique in psalmody, is

136 where the second half of every verse proclaims 'for his mercy endureth for ever'. This in some respects mirrors the Benedicite, although that is not psalmody in the accepted sense.

It is not always realized that the psalter is divided into five separate and distinct books, each of which ends with a doxology of praise. These are 1–41, 42–72, 73–89, 90–106 and 107–150, the final four psalms (147–150) being something of an extended doxology to the entire psalter with shades of the Benedicite re-echoed in 147, and especially in 148.

From all this it will be realized that the marriage of suitable chants is crucial if psalms are to be musically enriched. While the choice of minor chants for penitential psalms and major ones for psalms of praise is a good general pointer this is by no means mandatory, nor always desirable. What does matter is the quality of chant, with the tempo and dynamics suited to the overall effect. Very few psalms have chants specifically identified with them in the way that many hymns are unthinkable without the tune associated with them.

I would suggest that choir directors study the words of the psalms in depth (there are many excellent commentaries available), and then convey the results to their singers. All concerned may well be surprised at just how varied, revealing, and interesting the psalms are. They will then see better the power which music has in carrying the words that stage further. This power of the fusion of words and music can be realized right across the board, even in minuscule examples such as 15 (note the summing-up in the last verse), 23, a clutch from 120 to 125, and not least the shortest psalm of all, the two verses of 117. Then there are the great epic psalms – 18, 78 and 106, usually heard only in cathedrals. Here the moods are constantly changing, section by section. Be it penitence, praise, the lament of the exiles, pilgrimage, or the twenty-two eight-verse sections of 119, each concentrating on a different aspect of the keeping of commandments, the plethora of subjects demands much thought and vision, but how exciting this can be. It certainly scotches the old concept of a uniform pace, come what may, which was once meted out to every psalm, in much the same way as many an organist years ago settled on one speed, and one only, for every hymn. But, happily, we have moved on from that position, for in the final count no two psalms are alike, or consistent, in mood and therefore in dynamics. How challenging this is.

While it may be easy to pay tacit lip service to these considerations, ultimately it is the singing and accompaniment of the psalms which must come from the heart if they are to be convincing, for every ounce of expressiveness and understanding is needed to relay to the full the infinite variety of poetry contained in the psalter. Without labouring the point, if ever there was a need for the spoken word to be enriched and beautified through the addition of music, this surely is it.

Musical Considerations

It has to be conceded that, as with hymn tunes, by no means every chant is a winner, or a masterpiece of composition. This can apply particularly to single chants where within the space of a mere ten notes it is not easy to make an impact: witness that of Pelham Humfrey, the melodic line of which consists of two notes only, and those linked with the Easter Anthems and Psalm 150, the latter before the advent of Stanford's fine extended setting. Is it then any wonder that Dvořák, on being taken to St Paul's Cathedral and hearing a long psalm sung to what must have been a particularly bad example of a chant, is on record as having commented, 'Why do they keep on repeating so dreadful a piece of music?' On balance, the incidence of badly crafted chants having to stand the test of continued repetition irritates the discerning ear.

On the other hand, these factors combine at their best to make chants which are both singable and memorable in their melodic contours. Herbert Howells likened a good hymn tune or psalm chant to the shape of the Malvern Hills as seen from the Vale of Evesham, the high point (the Worcestershire Beacon) coming three-quarters of the way through before a fairly swift final descent, as in Example 4.1.

Example 4.1

C. F. South

High reciting notes are not generally in the best interests of psalm singing, particularly when a congregation is involved. The addition of the right music is crucial in reflecting the mood of the words. Get this partnership right and you have a rewarding amalgam for singers and congregation alike. This can be particularly relevant in cathedrals where the daily singing of the psalms deriving from long usage over the years may for a listening congregation result in an experience which can be the highlight of Evensong. There are many possible permutations in the linking of words and chants, which are not locked into texts as are many hymns. While it would be virtually unthinkable to sing hardy hymn favourites at Christmas and Easter to any but the well-known tunes, there is no one chant universally sung to well-known psalms such as 23, 67 and 121 (though the latter gets near to it with Walford Davies' chant, as does Stanford for 150). On the other hand, it is no bad thing when a new chant is introduced to a psalm, something which the Editors of *Common Praise*, the new Millennium edition of *Hymns Ancient and Modern*, have suggested for certain well-known hymns, anticipating that both words and music will benefit from an alternative marriage.

In parishes, if the psalms are sung at all, they will probably be confined to a handful of short familiar ones, such as 15, 23, 67, 121, 122 and 150, often using well-known and readily singable chants. The same applies even more to the canticles which, although not psalmody as such, are usually treated in the same way in parish situations.

The Gloria

With its ascription to the Trinity this serves to christianize the Hebrew texts. In practice, the Gloria is often sung loudly, whatever the mood of the psalm which precedes it. A quiet psalm followed by a short pause, and then the Gloria sung reflectively, is as telling as a buoyant psalm immediately followed by a loud Gloria. Nowadays, in some instances, particularly when singing the psalms set for the day in cathedrals, one Gloria is sung at the conclusion, as has been the custom where sections of 119 are sung concurrently.

Interpretation and Performance

No other branch in the whole of church music is subjected to such personalized interpretation as the psalms. There are choir directors who contrive to distort psalm texts in idiosyncratic ways they would never dream of in Bach's *Jesu, joy of man's desiring* or the Magnificat and Nunc Dimittis of Stanford in B flat. Choral Evensong on Radio 3 on

Wednesdays can be a revelation in how *not* to sing psalms, as it can also be uplifting through its sheer beauty. It is extraordinary how virtually no two cathedral organists interpret the psalms in the same way. Perhaps this is a good thing, though it can have its dangers. In some instances each of the psalms for the day will be sung at a consistently brisk tempo, whether the words be joyful or penitential. In other instances they will be laboriously slow, with important words so emphasized and drawn out as to become precious, even bizarre, and surely a distraction for the listener. Add to this maybe a dull monochrome accompaniment and rigid, clinical singing, and one is forced to question whether such treatment comes from the heart.

Certain considerations have of course to be taken into account with a resonant building, such as St Paul's Cathedral or York Minster, which demands a broad basic tempo so that the words can breathe and be clearly heard. Diction, beauty of vowel sounds and clarity of consonants are, however, essential basic points of departure in *all* singing.

Pointers on Interpretation

1. Avoid the tendency to hurry long reciting notes and then to slow down for the subsequent chord changes. The most extreme examples come at verses 4 and 30 of Psalm 68, though this psalm is not likely to be sung other than in cathedrals. The most effective way of dealing with reciting notes is to sense a feeling of word and tonal growth leading on to the change of chord which often coincides with an important word.

2. Accentuation should be as in normal speech in order to bring out any necessary emphasis. By leaning on a particular word and making it slightly longer the meaning of the phrase is made clearer, and more helpful to the lis-

tener. For example:

> Psalm 32:4. For <u>thy</u> hand is <u>heavy</u> upon me day and night:
> Psalm 48:13. For <u>this</u> God is <u>our</u> God for ever and ever:
> Psalm 51:13. <u>Then</u> shall I teach thy ways unto the wicked:

This stressing of certain key words should not be confused with the generally understood musical meaning of an accent.

3. Unison can in certain instances highlight the word sense. This need not necessarily always involve the full choir and can be even more effective when higher and lower voices alternate.

4. The natural flow of words and music are a must, but without the inordinate gap sometimes made at the colon which is correct in plainchant but not for Anglican chanting.

Accompaniment

As with hymns, the play-over should set the mood and familiarize the congregation with the chant. The pace and the choice of stops should relate to the mood of the psalm. There are two schools of thought as to the way in which the chant should be played over. Some opt for free rhythm on the grounds that the traditional semibreves and minims are arbitrary and to observe them detracts from the concept of speech rhythm. This however can be inconsistent and off-putting. Others regard the written note values as a helpful, and familiar, rhythmic shape with a dignity of its own.

When a '2nd part' is indicated, some organists rush in with the initial chord almost before the choir has had time to complete the previous verse. Whatever the reason, this can upset the flow of the psalm.

It has to be borne in mind that the accompaniment is the icing on the cake and when well done adds enrichment to the whole. Where there is a self-reliant choir, as in cathedrals, the organ can add much in colour by providing a single melodic line using a flute or oboe stop like a descant weaving in and out over the voices, though if the singing is congregational some of these niceties are ruled out. Where the conditions apply, the full range of organ tonal accompaniment can provide some splendid examples of word painting. In confounding enemies, smiting their backsides and making short shrift of the wicked, all sorts of opportunities arise which an experienced organist can colour to great effect. In some ways this elaboration is akin to orchestrating the psalms though this should not be embarked on until one has had ample opportunity to experiment in private.

Recent Developments

Because of the inherent difficulties of singing psalms to Anglican chants, certainly where congregations are concerned, other ways have been devised as alternatives. The pioneer in this field was Joseph Gelineau, a Belgian Jesuit priest, who initiated a responsorial approach, the general concept being that the choir or a soloist sings two or three verses followed by the congregation adding a simple recurring refrain which expresses the theme of the psalm in question. By this method the more experienced musicians deal with the non-recurring material, leaving the congregation every so often to insert a short responsorial phrase.

The problem with Gelineau is the less than satisfactory translation coupled with the forbidding way in which the words and music are set out on the printed page. Probably for these reasons Gelineau's method has not caught on universally although, as with most pioneers, it did at least pave the way for others to benefit from and to build on it to better advantage. Dom Gregory Murray used virtually the same type of approach but set it out in a much more attractive and certainly simpler way. A number of his versions are included in *The New English Hymnal*.

The demise of Morning and Evening Prayer in so many churches is a further reason for the diminished use of the psalms, though short psalms and sections of psalms are sometimes used as an Introit in the Parish Communion, as in cathedrals after the Old Testament reading or between the Epistle and Gospel. A further alternative is plainchant, the Church's highly evocative folk music and, as far as psalmody is concerned, simple to cope with. Unfortunately, plainchant is still considered in some quarters to be either 'high church' or Roman Catholic, though in fact it is exclusively neither.

Reverting to traditional methods, recent trends have seen some strangely conceived Anglican chants with inordinately high reciting notes and angular discordant harmonies, resulting in constraint on their usage. Such examples seem alien to the traditional concept of a chant and its suitability as a simple musical vehicle for clothing the words in a new dimension. As with some contemporary settings of Versicles and Responses maybe this is trying to be clever for its own sake.

In summing up, how we elect to approach psalms, how we clothe them with music, and consequently how we sing them, is probably one of the most contentious aspects of church music with such a confusing number of methods, options and interpretations on offer. Resources, the expertise of choirs and the acoustics of a church are all contributory factors demanding flexibility. It is ultimately a matter of what works in one situation and tradition being out of place in another. But one thing is inescapable, the beauty of Coverdale's text, warts and all, as an ideal vehicle for singing and, following on from this, the need for it to be linked to the best and most suitable music.

5

Music for Holy Communion

Introduction

From the earliest days of the Church and across the length and breadth of Christendom, the Mass, Eucharist, Holy Communion – three labels for the same service – has been a unifying expression of worship. Its music has ranged from ornate double choir settings to the very simplest single melodic line, and with all that lies between. This form of liturgical worship has always been central to Christianity, even if at certain periods it was sidelined, though only temporarily. It is therefore hardly surprising that the words of the Mass have been set many hundreds of times down the centuries. They have conjured up countless approaches dictated not only by period – Baroque, Romantic or twentieth-century – but by an underlying individuality and vision, and with varying needs and resources in mind. After all, with such a wonderfully inspiring text to be let loose on, composers have readily seized its possibilities. It is therefore not surprising that practically every composer in every age who has written for the Church has provided for the Mass.

It is interesting to compare the different approaches from the earliest Masses down to the present day, though in virtually every instance these occur within a more or less identical structural pattern:

The Kyries fall neatly into three-, six- or nine-fold sections – 'Kyrie eleison', 'Christe eleison' and Kyrie eleison' – a ternary plan seen also in virtually every example of sonata and symphonic form in the Classical and Romantic periods.

The text of *Gloria in excelsis* falls equally naturally into three parts with a contrasted and usually more reflective middle section flanked on either side by much vitality and exuberance, with the final part ('For thou only art holy; . . . in the glory of God the Father') drawing forth in most instances highly charged music.

The same constructional thread more often than not applies to *Sanctus*, with a spacious three-fold 'Holy' followed by a more mobile section frequently concluding with a vigorous 'Hosanna', especially in Haydn and Mozart. *Benedictus* is frequently linked with *Sanctus* and concludes with an identical *Hosanna*.

When composers have included *Agnus Dei* the text yet again conveniently divides into an ABA three-section form.

Much of what follows surveys what is currently in use, especially in cathedrals and similar establishments. To a lesser degree the same considerations apply to recitals, though obviously the Mass is best, and most suited, as was the intention, within the context of the liturgy.

The Sixteenth and Seventeenth Centuries

During this period there was a great outpouring of Mass settings in continental Europe with composers including Palestrina, Lassus, Victoria, Hassler and Monteverdi contributing what in recent years has formed an increasing part of the liturgical repertoire of most English cathedrals and

collegiate chapels, together with those parish churches which
have the necessary resources. They are now generally sung in
Latin, these being the texts they were written for, and not
English translations. Much of this is austere reflective music,
some would claim impersonal, even clinical, a conclusion
which could sometimes be drawn from hearing performances
which lack the many subtleties and niceties required to bring
out the full magic of the music. As in many of the anthems of
this period, this relies in the main on the unfolding of expansive line upon line of contrapuntal beauty. The interest moreover is more or less equally divided between the voice parts
yet with prominence when a particular phrase sets a pattern
through a new motif appearing after a short rest, then getting
out of the way for other parts to enter. All of this is very
much akin to a string quartet where each part is aware of
when it has prominence or otherwise, sensing its role at any
particular moment in the overall web of sound.

For the most part the phrases are legato and call for disciplined breath control and tone, particularly as quite a lot of
the music is slowish in movement, such as the Kyries and
Agnus Dei. There are few dramatic highlights but many subtleties when long notes need to grow in intensity and where
focal points are created by the higher notes; these, because
of the equality of voice parts inherent in the musical scheme,
can as readily be found in the inner parts as they would be in
the top line in strict harmonic writing. Dynamics, which
may or may not be marked in the score, need careful awareness so that prominence where needed, and balance, can be
achieved.

As always, vowels and consonants will need care, the more
so considering that much of the music may be fairly slow
moving. Latin pronunciation is a thorny problem with pun-
dits always ready to air their views. I would suggest that long
vowel sounds, because they are richer and more sonorous,
are the best for singing, for example, 'Sarnc-toos' rather than

the flat 'Sank-tuss', and 'Ar-neuss', not 'ag-noos'. 'Excelsis' is variously interpreted as either 'egg-shell-sees' or 'ex-<u>chell</u>-seese'. As in all music moving at a moderate tempo, double consonants demand space if each is to be clearly enunciated – 'ga̧lore-ree-fee-karmus' (glorificamus) and 'pȩr-<u>lay</u>-knee' (pleni), not exaggerated and not hurried. Other recurring words include 'vol-oon-<u>tar</u>-teese' (voluntatis) and 'o-<u>sar</u>-ner' (osanna), which is best without a preliminary 'h' as in the Bach B minor Mass, the aspirate detracting from the vitality of the word.

All this, and more, adds up to how perceptively we elect to approach the interpretation of this kind of music so that its vitality can be rhythmically projected through the diction. English vowel sounds, by marked contrast with Latin, are less colourful. Anglicizing the vowels when singing in Latin is counter-productive and can all too easily come across to the listener as being monochrome, even dull.

The fact that much of the music of this period is for un-accompanied voices can present problems with maintaining the pitch; as with string quartets, it is a matter of listening not only to one's own voice part but to those round about. Chromatic notes, being foreign to the key centre, can be further obstacles, with danger spots being descending chromatics and rising tones, all of which must be carefully – and accurately – tuned.

The Eighteenth Century

What we have so far discussed is in sharp contrast to the profusion of homophonic settings of the Mass by Mozart, Haydn and their contemporaries. In these we experience exhilarating, effervescent, melodic contours – and not only in the soprano line – ideally with instrumental accompaniment. There are some sublime 'slow movements' where many nuances abound in Kyries, Agnus Dei and the middle section of the Gloria. The sheer inventiveness seen in Mozart, with more than fifty church compositions to his credit, including seventeen Masses, is closely pursued by Haydn, making the nett result of their genius the more remarkable and sophisticated.

Mozart sometimes uses pictorial motifs, as in the *Spatzenmesse* KV 220 (the Sparrow Mass) where the chirping of birds forms a happy and charming innovation in the accompaniment. Here, as elsewhere, his way of setting the Gloria, and particularly the Hosannas, is invariably full of fun, the musical contours dancing along in a buoyant way and as often as not coming to a sudden unexpected conclusion. While it mirrors much of his secular music, this is nevertheless church music through and through, never flippant nor out of place in the context of worship. When the accompaniment is restricted to the organ, as of necessity it frequently will be, the onus on the organist is considerable, the organ not having the bite of strings, wind and brass, the more so as many English organs are Romantic in design and voicing.

The Masses of Haydn, Mozart and others are being increasingly sung today in a liturgical context, this in itself something of an innovation to be applauded especially in cathedrals, and when sometimes using the instrumental forces for which they were written. How apt, and true, it was when Thurston Dart maintained that 'music is the bicycle on which the liturgy rides'.

Choirs and their directors can gain much from studying some of the symphonies and piano concertos of the Viennese composers of this period, the renowned slow movement of Mozart's piano concerto in C, K 467, being a particularly valid example. These can be helpful guidelines as to what was probably in the minds of eighteenth-century composers when a liturgical text was involved. In terms of the singers extracting the most from the music, and the organist from the accompaniment, the Haydn/Mozart Mass repertoire to a degree looks after itself, providing stylistic considerations are taken on board and articulation is neat, precise and even at times necessarily metallic. The symmetry and precision, while demanding a disciplined approach, nevertheless equally need a much more carefree light-touch approach when compared with the more austere Italian and Spanish Masses we discussed earlier. 'Why cannot I praise God cheerfully?' was the gist of Haydn's response to the charge that his church music was frivolous.

In all instances choirs have to be aware of the verbal context, the more so where Latin, and not the vernacular, is concerned, while the slower moving and more legato sections call for an expansively contrasted treatment if the music is going to ring true for the worshipper; such is the versatility of these works.

Though aeons apart in style and concept from the contrapuntal Masses of the previous generation, these eighteenth-century examples can gain in their approach and performance if they are viewed as the aural counterpart of the sometimes extravagantly ornate yet delicate architecture of the Baroque churches of Southern Germany and Austria, replete with their magnificence of colour.

An interesting contrast is provided by the Missa Brevis with the through-composed principle meaning basically one musical note to each word or syllable (as we shall later see in the music of Merbecke); this brevity is in marked contrast to the voice parts which unfold leisurely at considerable length. The Missa Brevis is also found in a number of twentieth-century examples, of which Britten and Kodaly are two commendable instances. An interesting parallel can be cited in the contrast between the 'Great' and 'Short' settings of canticles in the Tudor period.

Although at one time it was considered a Roman Catholic practice to sing in Latin, we have in the main moved on from this position and have hopefully avoided the inevitable incompatabilities which arise when attempting to accommodate a text for which the music was not conceived and which resulted in something of a square peg and round hole situation.

While not strictly within the remit of our survey it is interesting to note certain associated highlights, such as the poignancy of the Crucifixus in Bach's *Mass in B minor* with its ending which all but disappears into nothingness, followed by the great outburst 'Et resurrexit'. Equally magnificent is the resounding opening of the 'Sanctus'. By hearing first-rate performances and recordings, choirs can glean so much to advantage from the sheer magic by which Bach achieves his ideal of enriching familiar texts when clothing them with music. These are but two instances of Bach's genius in which we cannot fully comprehend the music without the words taking priority. The fusion of the two creates a rich experience. But maybe this is not a fair comparison, for the B minor Mass is, because of its length, seldom, if ever, heard in the context of the liturgy, though I do recall the Beethoven *Missa Solemnis* being sung liturgically some years ago in Westminster Abbey.

The text of the Requiem Mass, as set by Brahms, for example, rules it out for Anglican use, though that of Fauré may be accommodated within the Anglican liturgical scene, as can some of the Masses by nineteenth- and twentieth-century continental composers; those by Rheinberger, Vierne, Schubert and Langlais, for example, now increasingly find a place in cathedral music lists.

The English Tradition

Finally, on to the English scene, the needs of which conveniently divide into two main areas – cathedrals and parishes. As far as the cathedrals are concerned, Byrd's Masses for three, four and five voice parts are in some respects similar to the Italian and Spanish examples mentioned earlier, though less extended. While Byrd in some respects is more concise, identical needs apply.

At the Restoration the morning service of Mattins and the so-called Ante-Communion reigned supreme and continued to do so for a long time, with perhaps sung responses to the Commandments and sometimes with the 'Gloria in excelsis' being sung. This period saw a waning prominence, and consequent minimal incidence, of eucharistic worship until the advent of the Oxford Movement in the mid-nineteenth century, one of the main features of which was the revival of this type of worship, often together with the accompanying colour and spectacle of high church ceremonial. The unaccompanied Masses of earlier times and those of the Viennese composers had fallen out of use in Anglican circles, though the Church did not have to wait all that long for Parry, Stanford and Charles Wood, who were the prime movers in reviving and promoting every aspect of English church music while themselves providing for its repertoire in terms of twentieth-century needs. And what a resurrection this proved to be, for these three giants had far-reaching tentacles, and consequent effect. The list of their pupils is formidable and includes most of the familiar names of the succeeding generations, be they church or secular composers. Such then was the influence of these three who paved the way so that English music has never turned back.

Of the three, Stanford was pre-eminent in terms of church music, and although this is a relatively small part of his total output, it is rightly the area for which he is best known. Each of his settings of the Communion Service reveals individual insights into his interpretation of the text. Take, as an example, the 'Gloria in excelsis' in the C major Service. After an initial three notes on the organ the music surges forward in a rollicking triple time with no slot even for the traditional priestly intonation. In the middle section, although the mood is contrasted, the impetus is maintained; it is crucial for the choir to feel this impetus before reverting to the final short section, thus making the whole in ABA form. The music of the Sanctus reflects through its breadth the majesty of the words – 'heaven and earth are full of thy glory' – which calls for an entirely different kind of tone from the Gloria, for the writing here needs to be really sustained and generous.

Examples

Because Benedictus and Agnus Dei were not part of the Book of Common Prayer at the time when Stanford was writing, when they eventually came back into use he wrote separate settings of these movements for use with his four Communion Services. These continue to be widely used. The Agnus Dei, which looks deceptively simple on paper, calls for disciplined precision and unanimity, the more so as the music moves slowly, making the writing exposed. Any untidiness will be quickly, and prominently, shown up, be it merely one solitary voice out of line.

Example 5.1

Notes on Example 5.1

Bar 1. Sopranos must be ready to come in on the 2nd beat, with a slight build-up in tone towards 'Lamb'.

Bar 5. '<u>ta</u>-kest' needs a slight stress on the first syllable, with generous 'a' vowel sound.

Bars 7 and 8. The final 's' of 'sins', although a gentle consonant here, must come at the last possible moment before 'of' on the 2nd beat of bar 8 (and all sung in one breath).

Bars 10 and 11. Carefully tune the alto semitones and emphasize 'mer-' so as to avoid any stress on '-cy' which is the unimportant syllable.

Example 5.2

Notes on Example 5.2

Bars 1 to 5. These lovely entries, so typical of Stanford, as at the end of 'Beati quorum via', need a generously shaped *mp*, with the bass entry *mf*.

Bar 7. Slowly articulate the double consonant 'Gr...' with the note changes on this long word accurately tuned and timed.

Bars 11 and 12. Do not take a breath before 'thy' else 'us' is likely to be untidy. It needs a very soft 's' while all concerned must unanimously observe the rall. by carefully listening to each other.

Stanford wrote fine settings of the Creed though these are seldom heard nowadays. Its length, and the fact that it comes at a fairly early stage in the proceedings, can tend to overload the service with music at this juncture. It is anyhow increasingly felt that the Creed, as a corporate affirmation of belief and faith, should be said or sung by the whole worshipping body, so Merbecke holds musical pride of place both for its simplicity and its brevity. It is also easy for congregations to cope with. Even so, in cathedrals it would from time to time be a bonus to experience these extended settings of the Creed.

Darke in F never fails. Its very Englishness of sound and its quasi-modality make it a firm favourite, not least as it is within the capabilities of many choirs to do it justice. Apart from the Sanctus and Benedictus there are no word repetitions, though a lot of stepwise movement, but the high incidence of notes of equal value requires care in phrasing and dynamics, as in Example 5.3.

Example 5.3

heaven and earth are full of thy glo - ry

This is but one instance where subtlety is needed if the music is not to sound plodding or even monotonous:

(heav'n – earth – full – glory)

Care is equally needed with dynamics, such as at the start of the Sanctus. One seldom hears this sung as indicated, not least the pianissimo in all four parts at bar 7.

The Vaughan Williams Mass, much of which is in G major though titled G minor, is wonderfully mystical music intended to be sung without accompaniment and mostly for double choir. This is a demanding work both technically and artistically, not least in the many antiphonal passages where one choir is played off against the other. Balance, together with the need for expressive phrase shaping, makes this the sort of music which hinges on the interplay of each of the two choirs in a developed feeling for partnership. The whole is wonderfully atmospheric and breathes the spirit of the liturgy in a movingly English way, but it is not something to be lightly embarked upon. The *ppp* at the Incarnatus in the Creed, followed by *pppp*, are just two moments that demand considerable vocal control.

In an entirely different way Kenneth Leighton's *Sarum Mass*, also for eight-part choir, and written for the Southern Cathedrals Festival at Salisbury in 1973, was one of the very first full-scale settings of the Rite A text before it became part of the ASB in 1980. Here the music is highly charged for both voices and organ, as witness the Gloria. In the triumphant final bars the phrase 'in the glory of God the Father' is thrown about from part to part in an ebullient way, culminating in the word 'glory' sung four times in quick succession, syncopated for good measure and producing an exciting finale. The text was obviously deeply felt by the composer who relays in so convincing a way his exhilaration at the glory of God seen through Christ and the Holy Spirit. A choir and organist who do not sense the impact here, as in the Sanctus, will be missing out on some memorable writing. Like the Vaughan Williams Mass, this is a work demanding a high degree of craftsmanship and artistry. Even if some of us cannot attain it, let it at least inspire us when we hear others who can. In the process its influence may well rub off on us and inspire us to reach greater heights in simpler music for, as we shall see later, it is just as hard to make simple music sound convincing.

With regard to parish needs there is the never-failing

Merbecke. What would many a parish do without recourse to his music for Holy Communion? When Merbecke produced *The booke of Common praier noted* in 1550 he provided 'for every syllable a note', in deliberate contrast to the extended polyphonic music which preceded it. The mistake so many make is to sing his Holy Communion music as if it were plainsong, which it is not. He wrote his music in specific note values and it is therefore mensurable, as in examples 5.4 and 5.5.

Example 5.4

the   Fath – er   al – migh – ty

Example 5.5

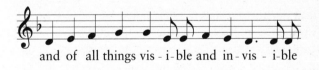

and of all things vis - i- ble and in - vis - i-ble

As suggested earlier, the Creed is sung in its own right for congregations to take their full part in corporately affirming their faith. Merbecke's music should ideally move at a gentle conversational pace and be supported by a light organ accompaniment. Other unison settings are more demanding, such as the Creed in the *Missa de Angelis* which is plainsong with at times quite elaborate melisma.

Now, four centuries later, with the growth of the Parish Communion movement, Merbecke has become popular, partnered since the 1930s by Martin Shaw's *Folk Mass* which he personally promoted in workshops throughout the country, producing a considerable vogue.

Midway between these and other unison settings with an emphasis on possible congregational involvement came simple choir settings such as Sumsion in F, not in any way technically demanding but very effective in providing attractive music at this level. Unfortunately, choirs have a tendency to sing simple music such as this in a routine, almost mundane, way, the more so when it is perhaps the only musical setting in use Sunday by Sunday. It is admittedly not all that easy for a choir to give such music a new look each week and avoid it sounding routine. An answer to this dilemma is to have two settings alternating each Sunday, or to have a more reflective and contrasted setting in use during Advent and Lent.

In 1980, with the advent of the Alternative Service Book, a number of simple settings of the Rite A text were published, the accent being on congregational participation. Richard Shephard's *Addington Service*, together with settings by John Rutter and Peter Aston, have played their part among others, and continue to do so, in providing simple and readily singable music. This is particularly important nowadays when often only minimal choral forces are available and the onus falls to some extent on the congregation. Perhaps inevitably, some of what has emerged is both pedestrian and uninspired, such as the setting by Patrick Appleford and others in the Twentieth Century Church Light Music Group, much of whose output here, as in their hymns, savours of the popular secular music of the 1930s. In some parishes dissatisfaction with what is on offer encourages local musicians to put pen to paper though not always with entirely successful results. Writing music is one thing but being a really instinctive composer with something to say is another matter.

One of the best examples in the simpler category is Martin How's *Music for the Parish Communion*, each movement of which is based on four notes (see Example 5.6).

Example 5.6

In the Gloria, congregation, and choir if there is one, sing the phrase in Example 5.7.

Example 5.7

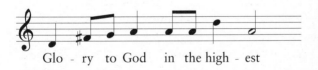

Glo - ry to God   in the high - est

This is followed by choir or cantor singing the subsequent non-recurring material alternating with the same congregational refrain through to the end. The Sanctus is similarly constructed (Example 5.8).

Example 5.8

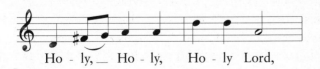

Ho - ly, __ Ho - ly,   Ho - ly Lord,

This type of responsorial singing has much to commend in it for it provides a unifying force involving all concerned, while leaving the congregation with a simple recurring phrase they can easily cope with. Congregations properly encouraged can make their refrain exciting, and anything but a 'vain repetition'.

Kenneth Leighton's service in D is a unison setting with optional SATB choir parts, making this highly attractive music and easily adaptable to most situations. Even when sung in unison it sends out a full-blooded message yet with the minimum of fuss. Its considerable brevity is a bonus factor, making this music which needs to be more widely known as much in cathedrals as in parish churches.

Finally, rehearsals for congregations are admirable, but only if taken by a person with the ability and charisma to draw out the best from people often reluctant to be rehearsed.

6

Canticles

Introduction

This is a wonderfully rich area with magnificent texts which have understandably inspired composers of every generation, yet this repertoire is little used except in cathedrals and those churches with the resources and expertise to cope adequately. Sung weekday Mattins in cathedrals is virtually a thing of the past, forced out through the priority of educational demands in choir schools and the inability of lay clerks to be absent from their place of work. Today, fewer cathedrals than ever regularly sing Mattins on Sundays. The demise of these choral services is a sad loss, the more so when weekdays gave us the chance to hear the 'Great' and 'Short' Services of the Tudor composers and similar more extended works.

What follows is intended as a representative cross-section of some of the finest examples employing a variety of styles and approaches.

Morning Canticles

Howells: COLLEGIUM REGALE TE DEUM. This was the first in a series of morning and evening canticles written specifically for certain cathedrals and collegiate chapels. It was, as Christopher Palmer says in his biography of Howells, 'a landmark for both Howells and church music'.[1] This Te

Deum surges on from its very outset, as a great paean of praise employing a basically harmonic style effectively interspersed with moments when individual voice parts are highlighted, as in Example 6.1. There are some sudden and most impressive changes in tonality (Example 6.2). At the end of

Example 6.1

Example 6.2

the second main section the extended treatment of the text provides a memorable running-down in both notes and dynamics. The culmination of many finely inspired moments comes on the very last page of all where Howells relentlessly hammers home as a grand finale the significance of the text. This is the sort of music which can readily send shivers down the spine and which demands that the singers keep up the momentum to the very end – and then to have something in reserve for the crescendo on the final note, having given due emphasis to 'trusted' and confounded (Example 6.3). The intensity of the music throughout, and particularly in these closing bars, demands a commitment and vigour from each

Example 6.3

Cambridge. Nov. 1944

and every singer not only to draw out to the full the dynamic colour content, which is extremely wide-ranging, but to shape and control the long phrases – and some of them are very long – underlined by richly sustained vowel sounds. This Te Deum, bound together by motifs such as were developed earlier by Stanford, is painted on a big canvas. Although relentlessly hard work for the singers, it is nevertheless so rewarding for each voice part, and not least in the contrasts provided by the strength of the unison passages.

Stanford: TE DEUM IN C. Of his five sets of morning and evening canticles, Stanford regarded this, his last, as his best, a viewpoint widely endorsed. Much of it is built on a simple diatonic phrase, four notes up and four down, a motif he employed elsewhere in the canticles in this key. Though less technically demanding than Howells for both singers and organ, artistically it requires vision and insight with emphasis on the shaping of broad legato phrases which are often built on notes of equal value, unlike the long melismatic phrases on single vowels used a generation later by Howells. After an arresting no-nonsense first phrase Stanford achieves a colour-ful crowd-like effect at 'the heavens and all the powers therein', followed by a three-fold 'Holy' beginning *mf* and building up to *forte*, then culminating in *ff* with all guns firing at 'Heaven and earth are full of thy glory'. This impres-sively grand introductory section is at times almost operatic. The phrase shapes and the dynamics set the scene for what is to follow and need, as throughout the Te Deum, to be faith-fully followed, and sensed, by the musicians. The contrasted Alla Marcia section moves more briskly with the text and musical interest shared between the voices. This is such grand music and needs a generously full-toned treatment, especially at the many key moments such as 'Thou art the King of Glory, O Christ', and the later mixture of unison and harmony cumulatively building up to the final utterance, 'Let me never be confounded'. The contours overall present an ever-changing panorama in which choir and organist will hopefully be moved to exuberance. If not, then little else will inspire their efforts. This is a memorable example of one of the Church's great historic texts further enriched by the addition of music.

Stanford: JUBILATE IN C. In mood and approach this from the outset admirably partners the Te Deum though with its own personality. It moves briskly ($\quad$ = 144) with the effervescence of the words matched by the vitality of choral tone needed to shape the onward movement. The music is skilfully coupled to the urgency of the words. This also makes a good anthem in its own right.

Britten: TE DEUM IN C. This is an early work written while the composer was a teenager. In its highly-geared originality it was a forecast of things to come. The initial two pages are built throughout on a quiet chord of C major with a recurrent pedal motif for the organ which is basic to the architecture of the whole. A magical moment comes at 'Thou are the King of Glory, O Christ', sung *pp* by a lone soprano with the full choir reiterating 'Christ' *ppp* (and Britten obviously meant exactly that dynamic). This is indicative of the control, subtlety, and imagination which undergirds this remarkably mature work, and particularly so in grading the dynamics. Discipline and team work is needed in the cut-off of final consonants such as 'Christ' where even one solitary singer out of step, however slightly, can distract from the effect. Overall, and not least in the sublime final bars, this is such a well-crafted work, and so different from the ambience of the Stanford Te Deum just discussed where the general shape and tonal range are achieved in the main through long romantic phrases. In the Britten the singers have constantly to change tone, style and, not least, mood. It is quite remarkable what can be done with the chord of C major.

Britten: JUBILATE IN C. Composed for the Duke of Edinburgh and the choir of St George's Chapel, Windsor Castle, and written many years after the Te Deum, this is totally different in concept, mood and, above all else, in rhythmic ingenuity. The Jubilate sails on with a relentlessly full-blooded busy effervescence. But how easy it is to be slack over the initial phrase which occurs again and again (Example 6.4). Here the first two notes need to be as

Example 6.4

O   be   joy - ful

detached and brittle as 'joyful' should be legato with a stress on the first syllable. The distinctive dotted note will benefit from being virtually double-dotted, and never given short value. The rests are integral to the overall concept and design, while unanimity must be assured in the release of final consonants preceding rests. All this contrasts forcibly with the phrases where legato is called for. The middle section, 'Be thankful unto him', is marked 'very quietly' and is virtually speech rhythm though written in mensurable notation. The Gloria is an exciting finale to an already exciting piece. It uses rhythms similar to those employed earlier, with a quiet 'world without end. Amen' underlined by splendid harmonies which call for careful chording, the organ giving virtually no help. Then, when you think all is

over, come a dozen bars of repeated Amens sung loudly, the
organ having the last say with a helter-skelter descending
scale passage.

In both the Te Deum and the Jubilate Britten showed new
approaches in setting these texts; they are further examples
of how words can be enriched to advantage.

Vaughan Williams: TE DEUM IN G. Spelt out in his charac-
teristically modal vein, this highly personalized work carries
the unmistakable hallmarks of the composer. It so admirably
underlines the mood of grandeur and occasion often called
for in a Te Deum, and no doubt particularly so for the
enthronement of Cosmo Gordon Lang as Archbishop of
Canterbury, for which it was written in 1928. The contrast
between the arresting unison at the start and the two SATB
choirs played off antiphonally against each other provides
the same sense of urgency and excitement as does much of
the writing of Monteverdi four hundred years previously
when he used the ambience of St Mark's, Venice to such
good and similar effect. The mood and pulse of the Vaughan
Williams are continually changing and are guaranteed to
keep the musicians on their toes through the urgency of
much of the writing. Later on this is exchanged for an expansive $\frac{6}{4}$ while the conclusion is a particularly beautiful instance
of how double choir writing can be so rich and effective,
especially for ecclesiastical needs. For the singers and organist it is basically a matter of highlighting to effect the contrast
between the breadth and warm tone called for in the unison
passages and the richly moulded double choir and eight-part
sections.

BENEDICTUS. Settings of this canticle are heard even less
today than the Te Deum and Jubilate, maybe partly because
of its length, and the fact that it follows a necessarily
substantial Te Deum. Gone, alas, are the days when the

Benedictus of Harwood in A flat was sung at St George's Chapel, Windsor Castle, during my years there as assistant organist. I cherish the memory of the final bars, 'and to guide our feet into the way of peace', for they are truly magical and exemplary of Edwardian choral writing for the Church at an inspired level.

BENEDICITE. Directed for use during Advent and Lent as an optional alternative to the Te Deum, this effervescent canticle seems on the face of it to be a strange and somewhat out of place choice during these penitential seasons. Purcell wrote a fine setting, if fairly long and severe, when compared with contemporary examples by Francis Jackson, William Harris, Herbert Sumsion and Robert Ashfield, all of which are propelled along with an abundance of interest, vocally, harmonically and rhythmically. All have fine stylish accompaniments calling for average technical demands.

The LAMENTATION of Bairstow, which will be discussed in Chapter 9, is a highly effective alternative to the Benedicite.

VENITE. Traditionally, because of its invitatory emphasis, this is the first canticle of Mattins, either in full or the first seven verses only. It is usually sung to a chant, which is no bad thing as Mattins provides for a number of lengthy canticles which *en bloc* can all too easily overload the Office with psalmody and make it somewhat indigestible. One exception worth considering as an alternative is the full-length setting by Anthony Piccolo, an American composer born in 1953. The nature of the words means that they are usually sung and played in a fairly robust way but Piccolo does the very opposite, and to good effect. 'Treading lightly' is his apposite direction at the outset. The dancelike treatment, basically *p* or *pp* throughout, apart from a couple of brief *mf* phrases, is underlined by a delightful though discreet quaver accompaniment above long pedal points. All this combines to single out this vibrant canticle as having new insight for singers and congregations alike. The entire concept demands extreme subtlety and control and deserves to be better known, though it is included in *The New Church Anthem Book* (Oxford University Press).

All the morning canticles so far discussed can always be sung in their own right as anthems, not least in those cathedrals and churches where Mattins is no longer sung. What better than the Te Deum sung at the end of Evensong on Easter Day as a culminating finale to a day on which praise and thanksgiving is of the essence?

Evening Canticles

As most cathedrals and collegiate establishments sing Evensong, as do a number of parish churches, a wide range of music is available and in frequent use. This repertoire ranges from Elizabethan times, or even earlier, to the present day, as a glance at cathedral music lists will show. A century ago the repertoire was underlined in many instances by constant use of a restricted range of settings. Many of them were Victorian and have long since been abandoned as they were of dubious quality, frequently an uninspired succession of chords of equal value which plodded on relentlessly with little melodic interest, and even less imaginative harmonic input. Rhythmic variety as such was virtually non-existent. This however was the prevailing taste of the time when much of the repertoire of the Tudor composers was either out of vogue or yet to be rediscovered by scholars such as E. H. Fellowes.

We have now progressed by leaps and bounds and can rejoice in the breadth of vision and inspiration which composers have injected into setting these texts. What follows is a personal representative cross-section which emphasizes some of this variety and its worth.

Gibbons: SHORT SERVICE is so called because there is virtually no repetition of text and it is therefore more concise than a 'Great' Service written for the most part in extended polyphony. This setting is best when moving at around ♩ = 100. There must be no hurrying of quavers, the words taking precedence and dictating the movement in phrases such as Example 6.5.

Example 6.5

The rare moments when there are imitative entries are an opportunity for contrasted rhythmically marked articulation, while at Example 6.6 Gibbons indulges in momentary word painting with a low E flat on 'down'.

Example 6.6

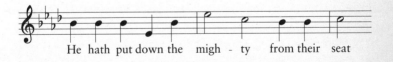

A firm tone with phrases sung in one breath will be helpful. In the Nunc Dimittis the alto line is for much of the way in strict canon at the fourth with the treble, a rare extended instance at this time. In the Amen there are charming

flourishes for sopranos and altos. A light beat throughout –
and in minims rather than endless crotchets – will help the
flow, for this is in some ways akin to vocal chamber music.

DYSON IN D. This has sometimes been considered pagan
music. I would not know whether Dyson subscribed to the
Christian faith or not, but I do know that this is a most
colourful, exciting and in many ways unusual approach to
the text. It is in most respects highly original, and frequently
exhilarating. The music does virtually everything you would
not expect in setting these words, yet it comes off.

By comparison, STANFORD'S EVENING SERVICE IN G
is completely different with its gentle contours and gloriously
romantic treble solo dominating the scene in the Magnificat
to which the choir from time to time adds equally gentle
comments, while the organ dances along in a succession of
quavers. Kenneth Long rates this as 'perhaps the loveliest of
all settings of this canticle'.[2]

But, to revert to Dyson's account, this is anything but ethereal, except in the Nunc Dimittis. 'Allegro con spirito' just
about sums it up. Who else has set 'and holy is his Name' *ff*
with the sopranos on top A, tenors on top G and basses on
top D? Later, where putting down the mighty from their seat
is usually treated in a robust way, this is either *mp*, *mf* or *f*
(marcato). 'He remembering his mercy' starts off with a
gentle legato and as ATB take over from the sopranos it
becomes from here to the end one gloriously cumulative
crescendo. At the end, when he reverts back to the home key,
Dyson goes immediately to C and then, even more dramatically by a quick chromatic move (not a modulation), again to
D which leads into a march-like Gloria. By marked contrast
the Nunc Dimittis is the essence of simplicity with the four
voice parts in unison in quiet sustained lines with a fleeting
move to E flat. In the Gloria, from 'As it was in the beginning' through to the end, the voices again move in unison.

With 'and' on the first beat of the bar and sopranos jumping up an octave to D, this could be a danger spot but again, as throughout, it comes off, simply because the writing is so vocal.

Tonal colour and the many dynamic ranges are crucial to the conception here in an almost chameleonlike way, as also are the frequent, and often unexpected, changes of mood. Singers must have a wide range of dynamic notches to hand ranging from *pp* to *ff*, often shifting quickly, and not least a feeling for the nuances that lie between. Dyson understands how to write for voices while presenting us again and again with the unexpected, which however is never gimmicky nor striving to shock as in so many art forms today. Pagan or not, the underlying mood makes us think more about the words than many another more predictable setting of these canticles, and that surely is what really matters.

DYSON IN F. I have singled this out as nothing could be in greater contrast to his Service in D. Here a solo soprano bears much of the brunt of the narrative, while the organ reiterates a gentle syncopated rhythmic figure as a background. The same sort of thing happens in the Nunc Dimittis, this time with a bass solo, yet the two canticles are quite different in timbre, if not dissimilar in mood. Everything throughout is restrained, delicate, and beautifully moulded. It is as if the composer were emphasizing to us that here are two quite distinctive ways of subtly saying the same thing.

In a similar vein of simplicity, Sydney Watson's setting in E (which he always referred to as 'Me in E') is a most effective work which says all it has to with the minimum of notes and fuss, yet demands a similar simplicity and gentleness from the musicians.

STANFORD IN B FLAT. A quote from Kenneth Long is a useful starter:

As a church musician Stanford is acknowledged to be one of the most significant composers since Blow. He understood the true function of music in worship; he was a man of excellent taste, he had a natural gift for melody coupled with first-class technical skill, and he was a big enough person to cut right across the fashions and styles of his day.[2]

The B flat service is so well known and so frequently sung that the full impact of the contrasts in mood and colour are not always arrived at in performance. It is all too easy to approach the music in a routine way; the fact that it is not all that technically demanding can lead to an almost casual approach. As with so much reasonably simple music it is a matter of *how* it is performed and the consequent impact it makes on the worshipper. Sometimes the Magnificat is taken too fast and becomes an ersatz quick waltz which denies it a dignified shaping. It will help to think of it as moving at one dotted minim to the bar rather than a vigorous three-in-a-bar. (This fault is made the more obvious when conductors beat a fussy three, the old adage that the fewer the beats the more the music flows being very much a truism.) By doing this a convincing interpretation will immediately be communicated. This will be helped when the conductor, if there is one, or else somebody in the choir wagging a finger, gives a preliminary initial two crotchet beats for the choir to come in on the third, then to adopt the one-in-a-bar. For the initial phrase (Example 6.7), which is an admirable fusion of words and music, a crescendo in energy will produce a telling effect.

Example 6.7

My soul doth mag - ni-fy the Lord

In this way Stanford's 'With spirit' marking will be fully realized from the outset, the more so when the singers view this initial phrase as an entity, helped by a tight and well defined dotted note. Later, the pulse moves into duple time, or a firmly marked four, at 'He hath showed strength with his arm'. At other times the mood is more restrained and legato, though with so much crotchet movement care must be taken to emphasize only the important words and syllables while lightening those that are less important and avoiding any stress on 'the' on the first beat of the bar (Example 6.8). A tonal build-up in the final five bars, and thinking in terms of two minims rather than four crotchets, will all help. In the Nunc Dimittis, although it is $\frac{2}{2}$, the feeling here is more of a $\frac{4}{4}$, pulse. Changing to a well-marked two-in-a-bar at 'To

Example 6.8

in the i - mag - i - na -tion of their hearts

be a light' and through to the end of the Gloria will contribute towards the momentum. When I became organist of
Exeter Cathedral I inherited a local tradition by which the
first part of the Nunc Dimittis was sung by T B only with S A
coming in at 'To be a light'. This served to highlight the
climax.

WESLEY IN E. Conceived on a large canvas this is not only
brimful of colour and interest but is somewhat unique for its
time in being sectional, yet, despite the inevitable stops and
starts, contriving to hold together as a unity. While these
sections provide necessary contrasts dictated by the words,
the performers need to approach the canticle as an entity.
The opening section paves the way with its broad and rich
legato. As an example of the sort of contrasts and variety
Wesley achieves consider Example 6.9, now in D major.

Example 6.9

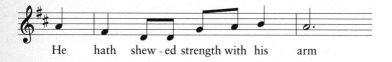

This calls for a detached marcato approach as each of the
four parts enters and will be better, and certainly less fussy, if
'shewed' is sung as one syllable – 'shew'd' – and therefore as
a crotchet. The robustness here is rather different from the
beginning and needs to be thought through in performance.
As with the Stanford B flat Magnificat, word accentuation
can go amiss if the first beat of the bar in this extract ('hath')
is stressed. But there is no problem if the initial word ('He'),
although coming on the last beat of the bar, is firmly

stressed; also 'strength' and 'arm', helped by a tonal build-up which mirrors the upward melodic line towards the pivotal word 'arm'. The final section, 'Abraham and his seed for ever', breaks impressively into double choir with some splendid vocal scrunches with the first sopranos on E and the seconds a tone lower. Why Wesley elected to produce so grand and memorable a conception for this particular verse is a matter for conjecture, though the end product is what matters.

Towards the end of the Nunc Dimittis and leading into the Gloria, all manner of chromatics emerge in order to get back to the key of E which is navigated through an enharmonic E flat (D#) for a couple of bars, making the start of the Gloria impressively highlighted. This is but one example of the imaginative originality and vision of Wesley, the more so if you glance at some of the now discarded mundane settings by composers such as Kempton, Travers and others a generation earlier. Here there is throughout the need to realize to the full the clear-cut well-defined harmonies and rhythms, for it is a longish setting and quite an assignment for the musicians.

It is interesting to compare, as we noted when discussing settings of the Mass, the entirely different ways in which these composers approached the texts.

Recent Trends

In viewing the church music of the second half of the twentieth century, Herbert Howells stands out pre-eminently, some would say head and shoulders above his contemporaries, not only because of what he wrote but how he conceived it. He started with the early Evening Service in G, a fine expansive work which unfortunately has to a degree been overshadowed by the clutch of twenty sets of evening canticles written for various cathedrals and collegiate chapels. As Paul Spicer neatly puts it in his biography of

Howells, these 'started to change the landscape of music for the Anglican church'.[4] Writing these undoubtedly reawoke in him his early interest in church architecture and, more to the point, the place of music as part of it. As Paul Spicer suggests, this consideration 'was later to become his principal creative force'.[5] What Howells came up with somehow seemed to avoid potential danger spots and to highlight and emphasize what many a lesser composer failed to realize. Spicer aptly sums all this up:

> What one sees most is Howells's sensitivity to language, and his thoughtful approach to the syllabic stresses in the text. Everything is worked out so that the words can be sung almost as if they were spoken, without losing any of their natural flow. Melismas are natural embellishments which allow us moments of ecstatic repose in the flow of the text, and give Howells the opportunity to voice the listener's own desire to be 'transported' at key moments.[6]

Other notable settings include those by Bairstow, where in his early service in D he write expansively, full of colour, vitality and flamboyancy, and also Murrill in E, equally exuberant but more twentieth-century in style. For the rest of the contemporary scene some of the best examples come from a handful of cathedral organists where, through long exposure to the scene, church music is well and truly in their blood. Francis Jackson, for many years organist of York Minster, has added immeasurably to the scene not only in his Evening Service in G but in his other work which extends to anthems, organ, piano and orchestral music, all of a high quality. There is also Kenneth Leighton whose Second Service is well wrought and expressive, with deeply felt vocal lines, contours and harmonic colour, qualities evident in all his music. Arthur Wills, who was organist at Ely, and John Sanders at Gloucester come into this same category.

Finally, mention must also be made of two early works of the twentieth century, fine double choir settings of the evening canticles by Charles Wood in G and F, generally unaccompanied, the latter entitled 'Collegium Regale'.

To round off this survey of evening canticles there are a number of simpler and less technically demanding examples which are no less searching in terms of interpretation and which, because of this, find a ready place in music lists. For example, and conceived in a traditional vein, come Brewer in D and Moeran in D, together with the attractive and rewarding settings in G and A by Herbert Sumsion, who was for many years organist of Gloucester Cathedral before John Sanders. Charles Wood also wrote three services in this category which, although fairly straightforward, are understandably attractive to choirs, organists and congregations. They are, as we say, easy on the ear, but no less effective for being written with the minimum of notes. Wood in D is an early work (1898), but one of his best, which he followed up by two in E flat. In all these the Nunc Dimittis is in many ways the most effective in terms of quiet atmosphere and especially in well-shaped melodic lines. These are but a few of the settings rightly popular in cathedrals and those churches where adequate resources exist.

The influence of S. S. Wesley and Stanford, both pioneers who had much vision, expertise, and experience at their fingertips, initiated the way for a much-needed spring clean and a new look. Their church music was a stimulus to later composers who gave these texts new life, colour and dimension through their compositions. They are in the main refreshingly different from the all but uniformly plodding note-for-equal-note way in which many Victorian writers, often cathedral organists who merely dabbled in composing, put pen to paper. There may be relatively few cathedral organists writing music today but their work is in the main of high quality.

As yet there are very few settings of the ASB evening canticles, Peter Aston's being a notable exception. These modernized texts, as with the ASB Communion Service, do not generally seem to appeal to composers, in particular the more traditionally orientated ones. Kenneth Leighton, however, as we saw earlier, came up with a winner obviously influenced and inspired by these words, as did Richard Shephard. Philip Moore, the organist of York Minster, has set the alternative BCP evening canticles – Cantate Domino and Deus Misereatur. Though not ASB texts, these are innovations. These double choir pieces are commendably successful although, probably because of the rare use of these words, they have not found a publisher.

As we begin a new century the pace and momentum of change, which has affected and often radically altered so many aspects of life, is reflected in virtually every area of musical composition. This has resulted in some extraordinarily cacophonous sounds with composers seeming to strive to be different at all costs, through discordant clashes, seldom with a memorable tune anywhere in evidence. The contrast with composers such as Britten and Walton, or earlier with Romantics such as Elgar and Brahms, is marked. In many recent works there is no continuous growth, influence or development in evidence, for today it is difficult, as in art and architecture, to be genuinely original without resorting to shock tactics, even gimmicks, nearly all the familiar permutations having been virtually exhausted.

7

Anthems

Introduction

This is an immense subject spanning more than five centuries in England, with a high profile centring on the so-called Golden Age – the Elizabethan or Tudor period – and its prolific contribution to the needs of the cathedrals and their specialized musical resources. While this compositional flowering was by no means exclusive to England, I have in the main confined myself to English examples from each period, ranging from simple anthems and motets for small resources to the more technically demanding pieces. The choice is to a degree arbitrary though with an emphasis drawing out in each instance what are, I believe, helpful pointers, indicators and principles.

The Sixteenth and Early Seventeenth Centuries

Few would deny that this repertoire is chiefly, though not only, significant in the work of such giants as Byrd, Gibbons and Tallis, and the direct or indirect influence they exerted on a whole host of composers. Many of these, although their output may have been relatively small by comparison, nevertheless contributed some beautiful additions to the repertoire. If ever opportunities existed to realize to the full the objective of vocal music beautifying the spoken word, here once again they are, and in abundance, and motivated by such equally inspiring texts.

As a starter, Tye's *O come, ye servants of the Lord* is a miniature which is a staple diet of virtually every choir. On paper this looks, and is, simple, but it calls for a considerable degree of perception if it is not to be a mere collection of notes of more or less equal value. At the start, as its title implies, this is an invitatory. If you recite the words of the first phrase and then add the musical build-up to the last four words, you at once get the thrust:

O <u>come</u>, ye <u>ser</u>-vants of the <u>Lord</u> and <u>praise</u> his <u>holy</u> <u>name</u>.

Similarly, later:

His <u>laws</u> are <u>just</u>, and <u>glad</u> the <u>heart</u>.

Here are two distinct sentences needing the comma to be observed, while the double consonant on 'glad' ('ger-lad') needs a deliberate emphasis. Small though these points may be, get them right and the rest will fall into place, including the brief passages later on which play their part in helping both to convey the meaning and to shape this little gem. Never underestimate the intensity, which includes the dynamics, of what on first acquaintance looks to be a some-what mundane collection of mainly equal value notes to be shrugged off inconsequentially. For a change, why not sing this to the Latin text found in most editions – *Laudate Nomen Domini*?

Byrd: *Ave verum corpus*. This fourteenth-century hymn text has attracted a number of composers, as we shall later see when comparing this approach with that of Mozart and Elgar. Byrd's account, although not all that demanding in vocal terms, has some beautifully turned phrase shapes and part writing. The mood is established from the very start and in particular in the first four bars where the initial four-beat note should grow in intensity and expression as also in 'korpoos' (corpus). Although much of the writing is homophonic there is a marvellous change of key from D to C at bar 15, the more telling because unexpected. In the second section there are some neat emphases through brief imitations, such as 'O dul-chees' (dulcis) and 'O pee-yea' (pie), and a few bars later the poignant 'me-ser-rare-ray may-ee' (miserere mei). What a rewarding phrase to sing which Byrd contrived to set to generous and expansive vowel sounds. As always, accidentals need to be treated with respect, as when F sharp and F natural are in close proximity. And then finally the Amen with ATB having the last word while the sopranos bind the phrase together with a prolonged G. This lingering expressive phrase just about sums up the anthem which, because it is slow moving, will rely on the purity and warmth of the vowel sounds in, for example, 'ee-mo-lar-toom' (immolatum). On all counts, sing this in the Latin to which Byrd set it and which fits the music like a glove. Even so, digest the gist of the English translation. If it is sung up a semitone in G sharp minor this simple expedient will transform the vocal colour to advantage.

Mozart's setting of this text, like that of Byrd, was a child of its time, with its expressive melodic line supported by ATB and organ. Although Mozart indicated 'Adagio' this is too slow; and 'Andante sostenuto' is a better tempo allowing the phrases to unfold more easily. In the final bars the interest is shared much more between the voice parts, while carefully tuning the accidentals found here in some profusion.

Elgar's version is an early work and, as with Mozart, centres much of its interest on the soprano line, though here the two main melodic phrases, first sung by the sopranos, are then repeated by the full SATB choir. The dynamics are crucial in enriching the colour, particularly in the second half. A lovely seven-bar coda rounds off this especially effective miniature which, with its marked devotional approach, makes it a good piece to be sung during the communion of the people. As all the movement is unremittingly in crotchets, particular care and thought are needed in shaping the words while lengthening certain vowels as in, for example, '<u>cu</u>-ius <u>la</u>-tus <u>per</u>-for-<u>a</u>-<u>tum</u>'. Think of '<u>pair</u>-for-<u>rar</u>-tum' which is so much more generous in sound than '<u>per</u>'.

Whichever of the three versions is being contemplated, it is helpful to study the other two and compare how each composer elected to view the text through his music.

Gibbons: *This is the record of John*. The verse anthems of Gibbons are some of the finest of their time. This is one of the best, and never fails in its popularity. The narrative is given to a solo counter-tenor with the full choir underlining and emphasizing key moments in spelling out the well-known words of St John's Gospel. E. H. Fellowes maintains that 'the solo sections . . . furnish illustrations of splendid declamatory phrasing coupled with true verbal accentuation'.[1] This is in many respects akin to recitative, with the interest heightened by vocal flourishes such as that in Example 7.1.

Example 7.1

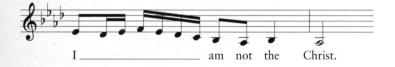

I _____ am not the Christ.

All told, this anthem is one of the outstanding examples of the period in this particular mould and one in which the choir, while playing a complementary role, do so discreetly and to good effect.

Byrd: *Civitas sancti tui*, with its more familiar English adaptation, *Bow thine ear, O Lord*, made in Byrd's lifetime, is on all counts best sung in the original Latin with its splendid opening section ('Chee-vee-tarss') (civitas). It is neatly constructed in three sections, the outer of which are in rich polyphony. This anthem contains so many subtle points, with so much colour and moving poignancy, as in the upward interval of a fourth or fifth at 'Ierusalem' and the repeated utterance 'desolata est' (and where 'dez' is more effective as the first syllable), dramatically underlining the desolation which was that of Jerusalem (Isaiah 64:10). In many ways pride of place must reside in the middle section cast in block harmonies. It looks so simple on paper but is intensely moving when sung with warmth and unhurried expressiveness. The profoundly moving atmosphere Byrd created is in many respects unique for this is through and through devotional music requiring great commitment from choirs.

In a rather simpler and less demanding vein come a clutch of small examples, all of them familiar as introits or communion motets. These include:

Farrant: *Call to remembrance* which unfolds in an expressive way with imitative leads in the first half which, together with the various quaver groups, call for broad and expressive treatment. The initial word 'Call' needs decisive articulation with an almost German 'k' (komm), while 'remembrance' is such a rewarding word to sing when each of its three syllables are spaciously articulated and in no way hurried. The second half is homophonic and has some especially vocal phrase shapes including, just before the end, a nice touch at 'but according to . . .' followed by a degree of emphasis at the phrase 'think thou on me, O Lord'.

The same composer's *Hide not thou thy face* is cast in a similar mould though rather more homophonic. Its reflective and restful mood demands that care be taken in blend and balance, which means all voices listening to each other as well as to their own part. There are to modern ears some delightfully quaint examples of word underlay such as that in Example 7.2.

Example 7.2

all   our ____ sins,

Both these anthems are 4-part miniatures of rare beauty and perfection.

Similar qualities are to be encountered in Tallis's *If ye love me*, though as with so many familiar and simple examples there is always the need to bring new insights each time it is sung. It must never be allowed to become mundane and routine, failings which can be all too apparent to the listener, probably more than singers realize. Though written in the key of F it will be much warmer in sound, as with much music in that key, if sung a semitone higher.

Making each and every imitative entry full of warmth applies equally to Mudd's *Let thy merciful ears, O Lord*, as much in the harmonic statement at the outset as in the part writing which follows. An initial phrase in simple block harmonies is, incidentally, characteristic of much of the church music of this period. As ever, it is a matter of relaying to the full the rise and fall of phrase shapes, both vocally and in the words.

Lord, for thy tender mercy's sake is ascribed variously to Hilton or Farrant. The composer relied very much on setting the mood in the opening penitential statement, again in block harmonies, before a change heralds looking forward to new life. It follows that words such as 'ten-der' and 'for-give' need to be leant on with due emphasis, as does the repeated final phrase culminating in an expansive, but never to be hurried, Amen.

Finally in this near-related group come two beautifully moulded gems. Loosemore's *O Lord, increase our faith*, with its charming emphasis on two-syllable words and double or triple consonants – 'increase', 'strengthen', 'wis-dom', and the delightfully quaint underlay of 'pa-ti-ence', a linguistic child of its time and such a joy for singers to articulate. The quaver and semiquaver groupings need to unfold in a leisurely way, while the extended 'sweet Jesus, say Amen' provides a lovely stroke of inspiration to round off the whole.

Morley's *Nolo mortem peccatoris* is a setting basically in English of a medieval carol text bound together by a repeated Latin phrase which translates as 'I do not wish the death of a sinner. These are the words of the Saviour', such a fusion of two texts being quaintly termed macaronic. Much of the part writing moves more by leap than by step, and provides an intriguing sense of mobility, more than might be expected in so penitential a text. There are some equally intriguing chromatics, not least D# against D♮ on the word 'painful', providing further evidence not only of word painting but of a somewhat unusual approach.

The Later Seventeenth and Eighteenth Centuries

Moving on to the next generation, three giants have due claim to be singled out as representative. Purcell wrote many verse anthems, as did Gibbons and Morley a century earlier. One of Purcell's most often sung works, *Rejoice in the Lord alway*, is known as the Bell Anthem because of the descending octave passages which form a ground bass in the opening 'symphony'. The narrative is for A T B verse, preferably single voices, complemented by the full choir contributing two shortish refrains *en route*. For all involved, and this certainly includes the accompaniment, a light and springy touch should dictate the style and mood. The emphasis is on the punch word 'rejoice', and is then more emphatic at 'and again I say rejoice'. Midway the mood changes, with a more legato phrase shape emerging as a contrast, notably at 'And the peace of God which passeth all understanding'. Here the suggested emphases will avoid any sense of a monochrome succession of crotchets. For the chorus, who are unemployed for much of the time, it is essential to feel pulse and rhythm continuously, even more so when they are not singing. In this way, when they are called into play they at once fall neatly and rhythmically into the scheme of things.

A generation previously this same text, which comes from the Epistle for the Fourth Sunday in Advent, was set to music attributed to John Redford. His approach to the text was just as much a child of its time as was Purcell's. Set for unaccompanied S A T B, the rising fourths in the opening section and again later add to the particular character of the music. Both composers make sure that the crucial word 'rejoice' is correctly placed so that the first syllable is on an up-beat, thus giving ' -joice' its full weight. It is advisable to make a brief cut-off before 'Let your moderation be known . . .' so as to separate more neatly the two sections. The closing is beautifully reflective and needs a real legato, particularly in the final few bars, whilst the earlier part should be generally more detached and rhythmic.

Purcell's *Thou knowest, Lord* is in a completely different vein. Sung at the funeral of Queen Mary II in Westminster Abbey and only a few month's later at the composer's own funeral, it is an intensely moving little essay, the more so if accompanied by four 'flatt mournful trumpets' as intended. The overall effect is achieved through the simplest of means. Phrases such as 'but spare us, Lord most holy', and the final few bars, demand a broad, spacious and committed approach to obtain the maximum effect, with the brief Amen an expressive coda.

To do justice to J. S. Bach would demand a book in itself, and anyhow has been done in various forms by a number of scholars. I would just mention two favourites, both from cantatas, *Jesu, joy of man's desiring* and *Subdue us by Thy goodness*. Both are cast in an identical mould, that of a continuously running accompaniment in semiquavers or quavers to which the choir add chorale-like comments separated by longish periods of rest. Here, as in Purcell's *Rejoice in the Lord alway*, the choir must feel the pulse throughout and not switch off when they are not actually singing. Too often we hear the very opposite of the singers coming in rhythmically and alertly, the more so in the second of the Bach pieces where each of their phrases commences on an up-beat which should lead on neatly as something of a springboard to the first beat of the next bar and the main word stresses.

Zadok the Priest must suffice for Handel. What an exciting work this is from its outset where the sustained and generous legato tone of the magisterial opening choir phrase is such a contrast to the busily effervescent and expectant instrumental introduction which precedes it. To obtain the full impact of this initial section the choir must project all the declamatory tone and diction they can muster, supported by broad vowel sounds, with the phrases increasing in intensity as they proceed. The following section ('And all the people rejoic'd') is diametrically opposite with its dancing triple measure calling for a basically detached approach, though care is needed in passages such as 'and all the people rejoiced', avoiding any thump on 'and', an unimportant word which comes on the first beat of the bar. Emphasis on the repeated 'rejoiced' needs to be cumulatively exciting as it progresses. In the next section a tightly controlled rhythmic articulation is of the essence from the outset ('God save the King') and then in 'May the King live for ever' where the dotted notes need full value through careful accentuation. From here to the end it is exhilarating fun all the way, though enthusiasm must not allow any hurrying. In the repeated ♪੭ figure at the Amens the quaver rests must be given full value; this can be helped by listening to the semiquaver groups in one or other of the voice parts or in the accompaniment. This will also steady any rhythmic deviation.

Battishill, although a mainly secular composer, conveniently slots in between here and the Victorians with two significantly large-scale anthems which greatly enrich the repertoire. *O Lord, look down from heaven* is, as Kenneth Long suggests, 'one of the really great anthems of the English church'.[2] The music here, which to an extent re-echoes the polyphony of the Tudor period, demands not only a sensitive and expansive approach but careful diction allowing the phrases to progress in a spacious way, taking all the time in the world. It begins with three voices and then a mounting increase of vocal parts and tonal warmth, though with significant moments of silence. One of these is a full bar in duration and serves to emphasize the text to great effect – Battishill perhaps had in mind the dramatic effect of the acoustics of a great cathedral. The anthem then moves on to a restrained ending. This is real vocal music achieved through the simplest of means.

Call to remembrance is a penitential anthem for seven voices, in the main homophonic though commencing in imitative polyphony. The second section, in the contrasted major key and in triple time, is written for three high voices alternating with a quartet for lower voices which is then amplified in the final section. This anthem, incidentally, is a good model for cultivating a really effective legato.

The Victorians

It is all too easy to pour scorn on Victorian church music, though sometimes with some justification, particularly in the words and music of hymns. This period is a variable scene in which we tend so often to highlight the bad – as, for example, the fetish of cloying chromatic harmonies and an all too frequent obsession with dominant seventh chords. Happily, as with Victorian art and literature, we are now re-discovering, re-assessing, and in the process finding the acceptable worth of the best of the church music of this period, though much depends on how it is performed.

Though the words of the hymns in Stainer's *Crucifixion*, as with much of Sparrow-Simpson's libretto, are the weak link, they are on the whole made up for by the tunes. One of the most successful moments is 'God so loved the world', perhaps because here the words come from St John's Gospel, but as with the bulk of the church music of this period the performance is invariably much better when sentiment is not allowed to creep in. It is all too easy for this to happen when excessive ralls. and over-larded expression marks take priority.

In the wider arena, Stainer's Evening Canticles in B flat are praiseworthy, as also the double choir anthem *I saw the*

Lord which is one of the few really successful full-scale anthems of the period. Although it commences majestically and powerfully, inspiration failed him latterly and the music tails off rather dismally.

Ouseley's *It came even to pass*, also for double choir, is a fine work deserving to be better known. Although something of an organ solo with vocal intrusions thrown in for good measure, it is great fun to sing and play, while the final Alleluias dance along unremittingly. As with the big Stainer anthem, Ouseley took advantage of word painting when it comes to the house being filled with smoke, giving vent to some dramatic utterances which are effective if not taken too seriously.

It is in the small-scale anthems that many composers of this period were less successful, and these, because they were frequently lacking in inspiration, are seldom heard nowadays. Stainer is on record as having said he deeply regretted that so many of his anthems had been published and that too many of his early pieces were written too easily. As Fellowes said in *English Cathedral Music*, 'in clothing magnificent passages' (many of them from the scriptures), 'he set himself a task which proved far too severe for him'.[3]

Mendelssohn, though not English, finds a ready place in the English church music repertoire, and rightly so. This is especially relevant of some of the shorter extracts from his oratorios such as *Elijah*, but with pride of place going to *Hear my prayer* with its beautifully crafted solo section 'O for the wings of a dove'. *Above all praise*, a particularly happy marriage of words and music, is as eminently singable as it is likely to be enjoyed by the listener. This is a shortened version for SATB of an Ascensiontide anthem and one of six seasonal motets.

Head and shoulders above all other comers, and in a category devoid of many of the faults noted earlier, are the two

Wesleys – Samuel, who was also instrumental in reviving Bach's music in England, and his prolific son Samuel Sebastian. Both, especially the latter, had a particular influence on the resurgence of English church music which was later to be concentrated around Stanford, Parry, Charles Wood and others. Samuel Wesley's *In exitu Israel*, another 8-part motet with Latin text, is a busily mobile setting of Psalm 114 ('When Israel came out of Egypt'). Built on four main themes appearing *en route* in different keys, 'Jordan conversus est' receives an electrifying full-powered unison. Later comes a delightful change of mood with a dance-like 'Mare vidit et fugit' (The sea saw that and fled) which could well have been written by Haydn. The 5-part *Exultate Deo*, frequently sung to the English words 'Sing aloud with gladness', is best taken at a spanking one-in-a-bar and preferably unaccompanied until the organ comes in fortissimo for the final phrase. This highly dramatic entry produces an exciting ending, but only if the choir have maintained the pitch during all that has gone before. Both anthems are high-class compositions, the more so bearing in mind the somewhat moribund period they encompass.

Wesley's son, Samuel Sebastian, has been rated the greatest English church musician between Purcell and Stanford, and with justification. During the course of his life he was successively organist of no less than four cathedrals together with Leeds Parish Church. He was an ardent and at times belligerent reformer; maybe this was partly why he moved fairly rapidly from one cathedral to another, for he was quick to tell Deans and Chapters what he thought of some of the existing working conditions. He fought hard for the rights and salaries of lay clerks and organists while striving for high standards all round. As something of a missionary and visionary pioneer, it is not perhaps surprising that his music stands head and shoulders above most of his contemporaries. His invention and his imagination in clothing texts with music may well have influenced Bairstow's dictum that song is speech beautified.

Wesley's considerable talent was exercised in an output ranging from simple anthems to what were virtually mini-oratorios, *The Wilderness* and *Ascribe unto the Lord* being two outstanding examples in this category.

Blessed be the God and Father was written for an Easter Day at Hereford Cathedral when only the trebles and a single bass (the Dean's butler) were available. Wesley later made this into the S A T B anthem we know, though it is easy to discern its original scheme. What resulted was a sensitively constructed quasi-miniature cantata. Because it is so well known and so frequently sung it must never be allowed to sound routine. The music is too good for that. In the opening section the crescendo is sometimes made in advance of bar 15, but this negates the sudden excitement of the resurrection and Wesley's obvious intention to highlight it. The extended soprano section 'Love one another with a pure heart fervently' was intended to be sung antiphonally between a solo voice and all the sopranos, though this will depend on available resources and abilities. The ensuing recitative, 'Being born again', is none too easy to co-ordinate neatly when all the tenors and basses are employed, as was Wesley's intention, the free rhythm here needing great care. As with many of the verse anthems of the preceding century, this one ends with a robust chorus heralded by a prominent dominant 7th chord, the pause over which encourages organists not only to pull out all the stops but to hold the chord down for so long that the continuity can be lost. In this final chorus rhythm is an important factor which, with neatly articulated diction, calls for a firm control:

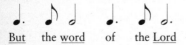

But   the word   of   the Lord

with full value given to the dotted notes. The final Amen will be
an exciting culmination if each pause is given four strict beats,
and no more, with the fortissimo maintained throughout.

O Lord my God, known as King Solomon's Prayer, is based
on 1 Kings 8. Although written in $\frac{4}{4}$ time it will move, and
certainly phrase, more easily by thinking of it as four minims
in a bar. There are the inevitable moments where accidentals
and resulting semitones will need to be carefully tuned. Here,
as elsewhere, treat accidentals with respect. This sometimes
underrated piece is also a good discipline in its need for real
legato singing. In *The New Church Anthem Book* (Oxford
University Press) there is a note on page 292 to the effect that
Wesley wrote two endings, one for boys and the other, with
higher notes, for women. An early example of sex discrimi-
nation? Singing this anthem up a semitone will enhance the
overall tone.

Wash me throughly is a similar example showing Wesley's
ability in setting short penitential texts. Beautifully constructed, and with an intense awareness for the poignancy of
the words relayed through the music, this is a wellnigh
perfect gem. Cantabile is the underlying point of departure
and what this anthem, shaped in ternary form, is all about.
The delightful chromatic clashes which occur between the
voice parts never detract from the subtlety of phrase shapes
at which Wesley was so adept. The upward intervals of a
sixth or an octave are all part of the scheme but need to be
accurately tuned, particularly as they are mainly in the
soprano line and therefore exposed. The middle section takes
on a more determined attitude in acknowledging sins and
faults, though here the longish sustained phrases are as
integral to the scheme as in the outer sections. Just before the
end the altos are given an intense phrase with a couple of
tricky upward and downward leaps before the final few bars

of long notes, each of which needs to carry through the phrase-shaping and grow in composite intensity. All in all, this is rewarding music but demands concentration to provide the cohesiveness fundamental to the concept of the music.

Finally, *Thou wilt keep him in perfect peace*. The choice of words from five different sources inspired Wesley to capture each resulting mood. This is further reflected in the changing musical approach: within only sixty-five bars coherence is achieved in a remarkable way, which provides a yet further example of how words can be carried a sizeable stage further through the addition of music. This anthem is by no means as easy as it looks on paper. After the initial statement the thoughtful mood immediately changes to a quicker two-in-a-bar for ATB. Just as suddenly the mood again changes back to the initial tempo for a re-run of the initial section though with different words. From here until near the end the urgency of the text ('O let my soul live, and it shall praise thee'), which includes the end of the Lord's Prayer, is mirrored in the music. Then comes the opening phrase for the third and final time, but with a new and magical ending, with a delightful clash of E flat and D in the penultimate bar. This neatly constructed anthem in ABABA form demands care by all concerned over the wide range of dynamics and the sustained soft tone; the final four bars should be sung really quietly. To relay the full impact of these words through the music calls for a disciplined control and an ability to grade the dynamics within the phrases.

The Twentieth Century

In dealing with this considerable area the world is our oyster and what follows can only be a mere cross-section.

Stanford was a wide-ranging exemplary composer the bulk

of whose output embraced symphonies, concertos, chamber music and opera, yet it is for his church music, and his service settings in particular, that he is best known. He was as adept at writing simple anthems as he was at more extended essays such as *The Lord is my shepherd*, a neatly structured account of Psalm 23. This is full of interest and variety of mood as dictated by the words, and food for thought for singers and organist. The outer sections are especially pastoral and capture the spirit of the psalm.

His three unaccompanied Latin motets were written as Graces to be sung before Gaudy dinners at Trinity College, Cambridge. *Justorum animae* is typical of the instinctive sense of melody and flow which underlines all Stanford's music and which places him fairly and squarely as a romantic composer. The double choir *Coelos ascendit hodie* for Ascension Day, though an exciting sound, is perhaps the least satisfactory; it inclines to be four-square and, surprisingly for Stanford, lacks full measure in inspiration. *Beati quorum via*, the most popular of the three, is a gloriously full-scale romantic piece in which advantage is taken of playing one voice part against another. What results is vocal music at its best, with the three higher voices played off against the three lower ones, the result something akin to orchestral colour. The ending is sublimely beautiful writing of much atmosphere. Each voice part throughout has rewardingly vocal lines, part and parcel of the overall picture. Howells once said of this anthem, 'Let that motet stand for works that by any criteria are not only highly accomplished, but profoundly human and of surpassing fitness.'[4] Correct pronunciation is extremely important, particularly in the two slower motets where long vowel sounds are so dependent on warmth and glow. For example 'Eu-stor-room arn-ee-may' (Justorum animae) and 'Chay-loss ar-shen-deet ho-dee-aye' (Coelos ascendit hodie).

Midway between the more demanding works and the

simpler ones comes the extended *Ye choirs of new Jerusalem* with its exuberant three-in-a-bar emphasis (and how Stanford loved, and excelled in, triple time). This is a triumphant resurrection picture full of the joy and momentum of the Easter story. As the mood of the text changes, quadruple time and minor key colouring take over, but not for long. Triple time again emerges for the final section with its triumphant Gloria now in $\frac{4}{4}$ time with Alleluias as a coda. This anthem is typical of Stanford's knack and ability to fit the occasion, capturing here the spirit of the Easter message in no uncertain way – and it is not all that demanding for the musicians.

Among smaller scale works Stanford wrote Six Bible Songs for soprano solo, each followed by a short anthem. In the event it is the anthems which are more widely heard nowadays, though the songs are well worth considering whether as solos or sung by all the sopranos. These anthems, which are generally quiet and reflective, are built on Scottish metrical psalm tunes. Two of the best are *O for a closer walk with God* and *Pray that Jerusalem may have peace and felicity*. To an extent these pave the way for the hymn anthem which has become popular, though some more successfully than others. It is a matter of what a composer manages to come up with while using a well-established hymn tune as a basis for a fairly freely constructed easy anthem.

As an example of a hymn anthem which does not fully come up to the mark take Henry Ley's *The strife is o'er* where the initial phrase begins, as does the hymn tune, on the first beat of the bar, giving a heavy accent on 'The'. The edition in *The New Church Anthem Book* corrected this and, where feasible, succeeding anomalies. Ley was not the only composer to fall into this sort of trap when the vogue of the hymn anthem was at its height, though most of the less successful and less inspired examples have generally disappeared from the repertoire.

William Harris's *Come down, O Love divine* is built on his hymn tune NORTH PETHERTON which he wrote for the 1950 edition of *Hymns Ancient and Modern*, as Vaughan Williams' DOWN AMPNEY was then unavailable, being the sole copyright of *The English Hymnal*. In the event, although it is of interest to see how each composer treated this lovely Holy Spirit text, it is in this instance the anthem rather than the hymn tune which has seen the greater use. This in a way is not surprising for it is a well-constructed piece, simply wrought, easy for the listener to take on board, and with the one deviation in the third verse where Harris briefly modulates and introduces a well-contrasted section using TB in unison. An optional descant is provided in the final verse. Because simplicity is the key word, this anthem needs to be sung and played in an unaffected way, while taking into account the various vocal needs.

The same composer's *Holy is the true light* relays well – and certainly enriches – a lovely text from the Salisbury Diurnal, particularly in words such as 'radiance' and 'unfailing splendour'. The direction *mistico* sums up the underlying approach and not least the generous crescendos and diminuendos which add to the breadth of the impact. The way in which he elected to set the text from bar 11 onwards results in the music being convincingly impelled forward to a climax in bar 21 ('gladness evermore') before finally coming to rest with a couple of quiet Alleluias made magical through the unexpected harmonies. This is music written with a real understanding for voices coupled with a convinced feeling for the words.

Two anthems by Parry, each quite distinct in concept and style, call for comment. *My soul, there is a country* is the best known of his Six Songs of Farewell. One potential problem in performance is the short sectional nature of the music which in the hands of a lesser genius might well have done a disservice to Henry Vaughan's visionary poem. For the singers, it is mandatory not to think of the end of each section as a stopping place, but rather as merely a brief breathing space while having the overall design and continuity in mind as the binding force. The changes in tempi and the wide range of expression marks need careful grading, such as the crescendo in bar 4 which must be significant so that the ensuing piano and crescendo can have full effect. Each section is best approached as a lilting two-in-a-bar, while the final and more extended section ('Leave then thy foolish ranges') calls for a fairly aggressive approach with consonants all but over-exaggerated. This will form a lead-in to the final build-up with its full-blooded part writing, while making the most of the final six bars and, not least, the crescendo on the final note. Whether or not the anthem hangs together as an entity is in the hands of the person directing it.

I was glad was written for the coronation of King Edward VII and has been sung at all subsequent coronation services. As E. H. Fellowes says in *English Cathedral Music*, 'As a piece of "occasional" music it could scarcely be improved upon. It breathes the atmosphere of magnificence that culminates at the moment when the Sovereign enters the Abbey and is acclaimed with shouts of "Vivat!"'[5] The opening, in both the instrumental introduction and then in the voice parts, is most arresting in its awareness of a sense of occasion, especially when all proclaim 'I was glad', making the most of the double consonant, and even more so when the word is immediately repeated; similarly 'we will go' in no uncertain way. The music builds up as it proceeds to a number of climax points, such as 'O Jerusalem', with the double choir section which follows a most exciting *tour de force*. The Vivats are part of the coronation ceremonial traditionally sung by the Scholars of Westminster School, and should be omitted in normal circumstances. Just before the end comes the beautifully crafted 'O pray for the peace of Jerusalem', warmly set in the key of G flat, after which it is a gradual, but so exciting, build-up to the end with the sopranos reaching a magnificent top B flat. An interesting feature which recurs throughout is the short accompanimental interlude in different keys which binds the music together as a sort of leitmotif, a device used to effect by Stanford and Charles Wood. The fact that this anthem is not all that vocally demanding, and is certainly exciting to perform providing you have the necessary resources, has given it an understandably popular place in the repertoire, though the organ part is not to be lightly taken on board for, as an orchestral reduction, it demands technical skill, and is integral to the whole.

It is always interesting to compare the way different composers elect to set the same text, as we saw earlier with *Rejoice in the Lord alway*. In the twentieth century Walford Davies's *God be in my head* is a miniature in which simplicity is of the essence, both in itself and in how it is performed. Despite its tendency to stop and start there is always the feeling of a spacious unfolding of phrases in a thoughtful way, though final consonants at phrase ends must be disciplined otherwise the overall effect can easily be marred. An important consideration is not to allow it to become sentimental. John Rutter's later approach, also unaccompanied, achieves its impact through different means, notably more ornate harmonies. There is a greater feeling here of unrestricted onward movement with the phrase shapes more readily flexible and leading on from each other. Midway, and on to the end, chromatics enter into the equation, and here in the bass line tones and semitones will need particularly careful tuning if the pitch is to be maintained.

Rutter's *A Gaelic Blessing* has words taken from an old Gaelic rune and bears the hallmarks of what makes this prolific composer's music so rightly popular as much for the listener as for the performer. The warm legato of the melodic line is allied to effective part writing in the ATB, combining to produce an atmospheric mood offset by a delightfully contrasted accompaniment mainly in running quavers. In terms of diction, the recurring 'Deep peace' demands that the two words be separated with the 'p' repeated, not 'Dee-peace' or worse still 'Deep-eese'.

Another miniature gem, Vaughan Williams' *O taste and see*, was written for the Coronation Service of the present Queen in 1953. Nothing could be simpler, though perhaps because of this and its strictly diatonic contours, it can be deceptive in its demands, particularly in the final bars, as in the need to retain the pitch. The composer suggested that it may be sung down a semitone in G flat and this is well worth considering as an aid to intonation. It is interesting to note that the initial four notes are identical with the beginning of his hymn tune SINE NOMINE ('For all the saints').

William Harris, mentioned earlier in connection with hymn anthems, came up with a charming setting of *Behold, the tabernacle of God* which, although composed for the opening of the Royal School of Church Music at Addington Palace in 1954, is suitable for any occasion and in any context. One of its great virtues is that this is vocal writing *par excellence*, underlined by long expressive phrase shapes and with a delightful brief excursion from the key of A flat to A which shows the artistry of the composer. It ends with gentle dancelike Alleluias underlining the emphasis on 'the joys of the temple with a season of festivity'. At the beginning, observing the comma after the first word 'Behold' emphasizes the meaning and makes all the difference in drawing our attention to what is to follow. The simplicity and effectiveness of the music here contrasts forcibly with the two large-scale 8-part unaccompanied motets for which Harris is particularly well known and admired, each with its awareness for what voices are capable of achieving in an almost orchestral way.

A contemporary composer by no means associated exclusively with church music is Peter Aston, among whose anthems is *So they gave their bodies*, a setting of part of Pericles' funeral oration at Athens in 431 BC. This short easy-on-the-ear piece for funerals and memorial services is a skilfully constructed miniature full of poignancy and greatly to be recommended. William Mathias, whose compositions similarly embrace a wide area from symphonies to chamber and organ music, is instantly recognizable by his highly rhythmic music for the Church. A typical example is the anthem he was commissioned to write for the wedding of the Prince of Wales and Princess Diana.

Two composers who have a knack for coming up with attractive simple music and whose contributions to the contemporary scene are of considerable significance are Richard Shephard and Martin How. Both have written for the needs of the parish arena. Shephard's *The secret of Christ, And did'st thou travel light?* and *Ye choirs of new Jerusalem*, are not all that demanding technically but highly rewarding in artistic merit, as is the music of Martin How, a popular staff member of the RSCM for many years. Two of his most successful pieces are *Day by Day* and *Bless O Lord*, the RSCM choristers' prayer. These two composers are pre-eminent among a group who possess the ability to deliver music which is attractively melodic, rhythmic and harmonic, and have done much to restore the art of providing simple music of integrity which to a degree was all but lost in the 1930s and 1940s.

The Continental Scene

Away from England, and briefly surveying the scene down through the centuries, much of the Italian and Spanish music of the sixteenth and seventeenth centuries, and in particular Mass settings, has been incorporated into the repertoire. This has happened not only in cathedrals but increasingly in concert performance by some of the highly skilled choral groups now in existence. If one is rash enough to single out one composer it would for me be Palestrina. On balance he excels in his penitential music, much of it for Advent and Lent, two liturgical areas which account for no less than one-fifth of the Church's year.

Bach of course reigns omnipotent, and while we tend to take bits and pieces here and there into the repertoire, how unfailingly memorable are the short 'Truly this was the son of God' in the St Matthew Passion; the finale chorale in the St John Passion with its wonderfully visionary words 'Then, waking from that dark abode,/ Mine eyes shall see thee face to face / In boundless joy, O Son of God'; or perhaps even more so, in the B Minor Mass, the end of the Crucifixus and then the electrifying outburst at 'Et resurrexit'. Even though these are not strictly within the context of this book, their significance and inspiration cannot fail to rub off on to all concerned and, I hope, equally to be an inspiration.

Five Examples

Finally, in a more demanding category, and as a postscript, are five contrasted examples of much depth and beauty, each having something special and different to say:

Bairstow: *Blessed city, heavenly Salem*. This large-scale heavily romantic anthem is typical of the originality and the vision inherent in virtually all of Bairstow's music. In it, and through its varied moods and sections, the organ plays a prominently cohesive role. This is highly pictorial music and as such demands much perception on the part of the singers, as it does of the organist. The score is fairly heavily loaded with dynamics and other indications but Bairstow certainly knew what he was about and these markings need to be faithfully obeyed. The section commencing 'As a bride doth earthward move' and the subsequent soprano phrases call for neat shaping and a sense of urgency through sharply defined articulation; a marked rhythmic impulse will contribute towards projecting the full effect of the swiftly moving narrative. This is then offset by the tenors and basses boldly proclaiming 'Bright thy gates of pearl are shining', which becomes the more urgent as 'blows and biting sculpture' intervene, through to the great central climax which is then taken over by the organ. As the momentum subsides the final section is by contrast gentle and beautifully crafted, bringing the anthem to a *ppp* conclusion. As this anthem is highly sectional in its construction, and as each section is so different in concept and in the demands on the voices, maximum effort in changing mood, tone and style is of the essence if the result is to be an exciting portrayal of a high-powered text.

Another Bairstow anthem, slightly less exacting but no less significant, is *Though I speak with the tongues of men*, a colourful setting, at times vividly so, from Paul's First Epistle to the Corinthians. There are many subtleties here in a text which obviously suggested much to the composer in terms of inspiration, for example in the lush middle section which spells out the attributes of charity, the word painting at 'whether there be knowledge, it shall vanish away' (as does the music), and especially in the final section which commences 'For now we see through a glass darkly, but then face to face' and where initially the voices are submerged by the organ. The final bars, with their insistence on 'charity', are a memorable partnership between voices and organ with the final 'charity' almost like a sigh.

In many ways this has much in common with Bainton's

And I saw a new heaven, a similar exposition of a fine text from Revelation with its anticipation of the new Jerusalem and the life to come. As with the Bairstow, full insistence needs to be directed towards dynamics and words, the latter being through-composed.

Harwood: *O how glorious is the kingdom*. This exhilarating anthem is in part almost as much an organ piece as it is choral. The arresting organ introduction is propelled along with more and more notes as it proceeds, before giving way to the broad initial choir entry in long unison notes. The contrast supplied by the middle section which moves in a slowish eight-in-a-bar is built on a soprano line taken up by ATB in a freely imitative way (Example 7.3).

Example 7.3

Clo - thed with white   robes __   they   fol - low the Lamb.

This is a lovely passage especially when approached as one long extended phrase, and the more so when 'Clothed' is emphasized by neatly articulating, and not hurrying, the first two consonants. This is followed by an even more expressive passage ('whithersoever he goeth') which needs to be accorded similar treatment with an element of word painting on the word 'follow' (Example 7.4).

Example 7.4

they fol - - - low

For the rest there is a recapitulation of the main opening section now truncated and ending on a sustained pianissimo.

Hadley: *My beloved spake* is the product of one of a handful of composers who are known mainly by one anthem for the Church, and one alone. Bainton and Harwood come into a similar category though the latter wrote service settings which retain a place in the repertoire. Hadley possessed an intuitive insight into the depth of meaning conveyed by this fine piece of poetry from The Song of Solomon and readily projected it in an almost flamboyant way for voices and organ alike. This is a technically demanding piece, almost angular in its melodic lines, particularly in the inner parts. There are a number of places where much concentration is needed in tuning chromatic passages ('the time of the singing of birds is come'). The rhythmic content is equally testing for singers. Add to this the thoroughly independent organ part and you have a sizeable assignment. Although perhaps for the upper echelons of those choirs able to do full justice to music of this calibre, it is nevertheless well worth studying if only for the various demands and complexities it presents.

Bairstow: *Let all mortal flesh keep silence.* What a marvellously conceived piece this is, using an equally gripping text from the Liturgy of St James. Every time I hear this anthem

I feel the four bars for divided sopranos and altos which come after the ethereal opening phrase for tenors and basses to be one of the most sublime sounds I know in all church music. The suspensions and the near proximity of high voices add up to a rare vocal sensitivity and awareness. But – what control is needed in those first bars, and then the release of tension at the more buoyant, yet still broadly sustained 'Before him come the choir of angels'; and the succeeding interweaving of vocal lines, much of it in stepwise movement and culminating with the basses striding forward and urgently proclaiming as the Cherubim and Seraphim 'shout exultingly the hymn – Alleluia'; and then the rests which allow for the echo in buildings such as York Minster and St Paul's Cathedral to have its full, almost theatrical, effect. Within the space of two bars the dimension drops from *ff* to *pp* with the lower voices reiterating the initial phrase, then with all concerned emphasizing in an almost ethereal way the final word 'trembling'. This is an anthem in which vocal sonorities are exploited to the full, but not something to be embarked on lightly for, while the music is greatly inspired, it calls for an innate and disciplined awareness for the words, and the need to relay them with conviction, if the musical result is to be of any consequence.

Postscript

So much church music, and particularly that of the Tudor period, was custom made, often, we surmise, with the acoustics of a particular building in mind – as mentioned above, a sizeable echo must surely have been in Bairstow's mind in *Let all mortal flesh keep silence*. In a similar way Byrd and Gibbons must have had Lincoln and Canterbury Cathedrals in mind when writing some of their greatest works, not so much perhaps for the echo element as for mirroring in ornate counterpoint the soaring architectural features of columns and arches, linking sound and sight together in a rich amalgam. Howells wrote canticles for a number of cathedrals, taking into account distinctive characteristics, acoustic and otherwise, as he perceived them; his well-known Collegium Regale for King's College Chapel, Cambridge is a particular case in point.

Factors such as these are not always taken into account by choirs and choir directors, especially when singing in resonant buildings, where articulation and quality of vowel sounds are of fundamental significance, and as crucial to the performers as to those on the receiving end. Too often congregations are subjected to perfunctory, even casual, sounds because the attitude can be the 'no need to spend much time on rehearsal for we know this so well' attitude, rather than the view that because it is familiar there is the need to search for a new look and a new dimension each time it is sung. The quest for new vision is, after all, the very basis of the mission of the renewal churches. Music, of all the adjuncts to worship, must never be allowed to by-pass these all too fundamental matters.

This leads us on to question again why some church musicians, professional and amateur alike, can be so casual in their attitudes when the finest orchestral conductors and soloists strive continuously to pursue the ultimate in excellence each time they perform a work. There is certainly no excuse for professionals who condone lax approaches, and less for amateurs who can get help from bodies such as the Royal School of Church Music. It matters not whether we are professional or amateur, it is the business, and responsibility, of us all to do all things well and to the best of our ability. Then, and only then, will we fully experience the power that music in worship can exert when it carries the words that stage further through the enrichment it provides.

8

Versicles (or Preces) and Responses

The concept of the priest saying something which is replied to by the people has always been endemic to Christian worship, the most familiar being the ancient greeting 'The Lord be with you', to which we reply 'And with thy spirit' or, in contemporary language 'And also with you'. Inevitably, these statements attracted music, initially simple unison plainsong as in the Sursum Corda in the service of Holy Communion, while the Versicles and Responses at Morning and Evening Prayer were similarly plainsong. Later these were harmonized in a simple and all but impersonal way for SATB or melody only with organ accompaniment. These are known as Ferial, to be complemented by a more ornate Festal version which was most effective but is sadly virtually never heard nowadays. Today, greetings and shared statements punctuate our new liturgies more and more, not least in the course of Intercessions.

During the Elizabethan period a number of composers set the BCP responses in a more elaborate form for choir use. Four of these, by Byrd, Morley, Smith and Tomkins, are published under one cover by the Church Music Society and have become very popular, especially in cathedrals. In recent years a number of other fairly simple Tudor settings have seen the light of day, with those by Ayleward and Reading being widely used.

While in contemporary terms some attractive versions have been written by Clucas, Sumsion, Sanders, Darke, Piccolo and others, some of the more way-out settings are ornate in the extreme and 'over the top' in striving for originality; Versicles and Responses should ideally be simple expressions of musical brevity matching the brevity of the words. Some, by becoming all but mini-motets, draw unfavourable attention to themselves, not least in the discordant content some of them promote. Some settings of the Lord's Prayer come into this category, and even more so the elongated Amens to the Third Collect which take a long time to say so little. They completely negate the concept of being miniatures, and while they may be an enjoyable field day for the singers they can be frustrating for a congregation. It is sad that even in worship, as in life in general, simplicity of utterance is a rare present-day commodity, as for that matter are moments of silence in corporate worship.

Two particularly effective sets are that by the delightfully termed William Smith of Durham, with its beautiful Lord's Prayer, and that of Bernard Rose, his being the forerunner in terms of setting a contemporary trend which in his case never fails, though good choral resources are needed to do it justice. Although the first two Amens to the Collects are written as equal crotchets, these can sound clipped if sung literally and are better if the first note is slightly lengthened and stressed.

In *Common Worship* and the ASB, as with other innovative services, there are a number of responsorial slots. Many of these are perhaps best said, if only because they are new and unfamiliar to many congregations who sometimes react in a negative way to anything novel. Some, however, can be sung to good effect if the music is simple and has the element of repetition as a help. Some composers in their Rite A Communion settings have included these, though with mixed success. The Acclamations which come at the end of the consecration in Rite A Holy Communion can be effective when sung; but it is more often really exciting if these miniatures are said by all concerned, boldly acclaiming that 'Christ has died – Christ is risen' and, most importantly of all, 'Christ *will* come again'. These three fundamental statements of the Christian faith are even more effective when the voices crescendo through to the final statement.

A further development, which can be experienced to good effect, occurs in the intercessions in Rite A Holy Communion when the last chord of the response is held on with the choir humming while the intercessor says the next petition. This can be a visionary departure if used sparingly on great festival occasions in cathedrals.

Whatever we opt for in terms of Versicles and Responses, a choir must be quick to make its mark, given so little time in which to enrich the text. At 'And make thy chosen people joyful', for example, urgency and a quick crescendo are of the essence, though not to the extent pursued by some composers who dovetail versicle and response so that the ensuing versicle begins while the choir are finishing the previous response. While some of the more recent settings show originality, there is a distinct danger that these miniatures are becoming over-elaborate, as for example an extended Amen after the third Collect. For the future, the musical resources and needs of the parishes should be borne more in mind and catered for. There is a real challenge here for simplicity in setting these simple statements.

9

Occasional Needs

Music in this category, because of its comparative rarity, can have a considerable impact by highlighting to great effect certain key moments within a service. As some of the more recent additions arising from the ASB are novel departures, and in many instances short pithy statements, often of a responsorial nature and coming after sometimes longish said sections, they are not to be embarked on lightly by the musicians. They effectively need as much preparation and forethought as an anthem, particularly as these phrases are not said, but sung.

The Litany

First, and with liturgical needs in mind, comes the Litany. If sung complete this can be a lengthy process. The Litany was the work of Cranmer. It first appeared in 1544 and today is virtually unchanged in the BCP version. In speaking of the Litany, Kenneth Long suggests that its words give 'classic expression to the thoughts and feelings of the worshipping Church and are at the same time incomparable as literature'.[1] Composers of the time, Byrd, Tallis and Loosemore, rose to the occasion with Byrd incorporating the traditional plainsong into the tenor line.

In the BCP version the cantor has plenty of variety in the number of sometimes longish petitions to intone, while the choir (and the Litany is not a congregational pursuit) replies

'Good Lord, deliver us' eight times and 'We beseech thee to hear us, good Lord' no less than twenty-two times. However alert and well-intentioned the singers may be, it is all too easy for these miniatures to become mechanical or perfunctory, even to show signs of ennui as the repetitions mount up. A well-trained choir will however endeavour to make each successive statement the more meaningful, for the Litany is so much better sung than said, especially, as in some cathedrals, in procession at the start of the Sunday Eucharist in Lent. The Litany is yet another prime example of how music enriches, however simply, the otherwise spoken word. These earlier composers fulfilled their task with simplicity, yet so effectively.

Lastly, using ASB and allied material, come recent settings by Philip Marshall (Church Music Society) and Philip Moore, the organist of York Minster.

The Advent Prose, Great Advent Antiphons, and the Lent Prose

These ancient texts are only infrequently heard nowadays other than in cathedrals and some Anglo-Catholic churches, and even here not with the regularity once accorded them, although all three together with others in an occasional category are included in the liturgical section of *The New English Hymnal*, as they were in the 1993 edition. At Salisbury Cathedral the Advent Prose is sung in procession each week during Advent at the beginning of the Sunday Sung Eucharist, as is the Litany during Lent. This makes a splendid devotional prelude to the service, as well as marking the seasonal element. Commencing in the far distance, with the choir gradually moving towards the congregation seated in the Choir, additionally takes advantage of what acoustics in a great cathedral can provide.

In some cathedrals the Advent Prose and the Lent Prose

are sung as anthems at Evensong on Fridays during the penitential seasons. All are set to plainsong but need a first-rate cantor who bears the brunt of the responsibility and, as mentioned earlier in connection with the Litany, a committed and meaningful choir response in the antiphons sung after each petition. On balance, it is preferable if the sopranos or the male voices in the choir are employed separately. It is less satisfactory, and can be less artistic, if the higher and lower voices are combined.

The Advent Antiphons, known familiarly as 'The Great Os', as each commences with the word 'O', are appointed to be used before and after the Magnificat at Evensong each day between 17 and 23 December. These highlight features of Advent.

The New English Hymnal makes provision for other occasions such as Holy Week observances on Maundy Thursday and the Veneration of the Cross, while the Sequences for Easter, Pentecost, Corpus Christi and other liturgical events are also included.

Lent and Holy Week

Additionally there are also

The Reproaches

Once almost exclusively within the domain of Anglo-Catholic churches, these are now fairly widely linked with, and sung at, the Liturgy for Good Friday and the Veneration of the Cross. The traditional plainsong version can be found in the *NEH* while a splendid full-scale setting has been written by John Sanders. This is available either in its original eight-part version (RSCM) or in a reduction for smaller forces in *Ash Wednesday to Easter for Choirs* (Oxford University Press). This is an inspired contemporary work gaining merited usage. It includes an optional organ part which is most effective.

The Gospel for Palm Sunday and for Good Friday

There are a number of settings, ranging from unison plainsong to that of composers such as Victoria in particular. There needs to be a really dramatic liaison between cantor and choir, especially in the crowd scenes where the temperature of the narrative dramatically heightens, and when in statements such as 'Let him be crucified' the chorus must respond with great urgency and conviction, all but shouting out almost before the narrator has finished. In this and in other similar instances the intensity and cumulative drive of the crowd scenes heighten the drama as the story proceeds, this being the *raison d'être* for singing the Gospel rather than saying it. Words such as 'crucified' demand for their full impact sharply articulated diction – 'keroo-see-fide'.

In this area mention must be made of 'Crux fidelis', a magical and highly original miniature by a seventeenth-century composer, the delightfully named John IV, King of Portugal. Its chromaticism, together with the unusual, though highly poignant, use of rests, and not least the text as such, mark this out as a Holy Week highlight. Its intensity, especially in the need for relaying with clarity the marvellous text, lays considerable onus on the singers, no matter at what juncture of a service this may be sung.

The Lamentations of Jeremiah

The intrinsic beauty of these words made them popular in England and on the continent during the sixteenth and seventeenth centuries. Not surprisingly they inspired a number of polyphonic settings such as the well-known version by Tallis.

One of the most beautiful, effective, and highly original

approaches was that of Bairstow. Written in the 1930s this is a highly imaginative realization of words selected by Eric Milner-White who was then Dean at York. Basically employing four extremely beautiful chants, the narrative is punctuated from time to time by a dramatically declaimed 'Jerusalem, Jerusalem, return unto the Lord thy God'. It is the sheer beauty of the chants and their appropriateness to each of the sections that marks out this unusual work in a very special way. Originally intended for use on Passion Sunday it is now more widely sung during Lent either as an alternative to the Benedicite at Mattins or as an anthem in its own right. Choirs should not lightly enter into performing this highly charged work without spending considerable time in rehearsal so as to be fully susceptible to the impact of the text, how to relay it and how the music locks into it. Chording, dynamics, and the need for careful tuning of accidentals and chromatics all call for a disciplined approach of the first order. It is best sung unaccompanied and with no sense of hurry, though the momentum is greatly heightened when the organ is used for the refrains. Here is a prime example of Bairstow putting into practice his dictum of song being speech beautified, for this is a real *tour de force*.

Allegri: MISERERE

In recent years this has become a great favourite with choirs and congregations alike through the annual broadcast as part of Ash Wednesday Evensong in St John's College Chapel, Cambridge. One sometimes suspects this is as much due to the understandable enjoyment of the exciting top Cs for sopranos as it is for the spiritual experience heralding the arrival of Lent. Because of commercial recordings by top choirs who make it all sound so easy and effortless, some choirs of lesser ability tend to assume that it is a fairly simple nut to crack. Nothing could be further from reality for it necessitates from beginning to end (and it is a long piece) not only technical proficiency but an intense concentration on both words and music if it is to be of any reward for the listener.

Easter Anthems

It is regrettable that these fine words from Corinthians and Romans which take the place of the Venite at Mattins on Easter Day are only sung once or twice a year. In those parishes where Mattins is still sung it is likely to be treated psalmwise, the traditional Anglican chant generally used being an extremely dull one by Pelham Humfrey: its melody consists of two notes (B and C) with supporting harmonies which are anything but earth-shattering. This fine text certainly deserves better music. Even in cathedrals where there is more scope there are but few settings, of which Ernest Bullock's is at least imaginative in relaying the spirit of the words. John Scott, the organist of St Paul's Cathedral, recently opted for a simple but effective chantwise approach which comes off well and is published in *Ash Wednesday to Easter for Choirs* (Oxford University Press, 1998). Whichever setting is used, thought needs to be directed towards interpreting the text which understandably oscillates between death and new life. It is important to avoid the sentimental Victorian ideal of violent contrasts, with life and resurrection being automatically sung *ff*, while any reference to death is *pp*. It is not so much a bizarre interpretation of dynamics as the need to project the words with understanding and musical conviction.

ASB 1980 *and Later Moves*

There is such a wealth of incidental material here that apart from one or two exceptions they can only be considered *en bloc.* As a result of the work of the Liturgical Commission of the Church of England and the experience gained in the twenty years since the ASB first appeared, certain modifications and additions have been tested out and in the main found workable and desirable. Many of these are short declamatory outbursts. Some are best sung, such as the Acclamation before and after the Gospel, either quasi-plainsong sung by all or slightly more elaborate harmonized versions sung by the choir for and on behalf of the people. The acclamations which come midway through the Eucharistic Prayer after the words of consecration, must be well and truly declaimed, whether sung or said.

There are a number of places where, after a prayer has been intoned, a straightforward unison or quasi-plainsong Amen is needed. This should be sung by all, but with a firm and decisive lead from the choir whether on a single note or not. If the cantor inflects the ending the Amen should have two beats only on the final note, and not die a lingering death (see Example 9.1).

Example 9.1

A - men.

A further instance where singing can produce a thrilling effect is at the conclusion of the Eucharist – but only if you have the necessary resources. Example 9.2 is an extended version for use during Eastertide.

Example 9.2

This concludes the main Eucharist on the great festivals at Salisbury Cathedral, but it only works because the Precentor projects his part in so exciting, even dramatic, a way that we are all impelled to respond equally positively, while we are helped by being provided with the music.

In normal parish circumstances these miniatures are on balance probably best, and more edifying, when well declaimed in a natural voice. As with Versicles and Responses when set to music, they need to be brief and to the point, otherwise they become too extended and ornate, losing much of their spontaneity and excitement in the process, as was suggested in Chapter 8. Whatever treatment is given them, said or sung, they must sound natural and inevitable, and never be mumbled in the half-hearted fashion which too often afflicts churchgoers. Above all they must sound convincing, for they are the response of the people which is integral to much contemporary worship.

Kyries

Liturgically, these should replace the *Gloria in excelsis* during Advent and Lent. Their penitential emphasis within the Eucharist is made the more real if at the start of the service they are sung between the Confession and the Absolution, thus giving people a space set aside for reflection and meditation whilst listening to music. This was the place anyhow assigned to the Kyries in the early Church. As with all innovations the reason for this needs to be explained to a congregation more often than not suspicious of change, if you wish to carry them with you and not alienate them by thrusting new departures at them without explanation.

Intercessions

On special occasions, mainly in cathedrals, with Intercessions at the Eucharist or elsewhere, there is a growing custom for the petitions to be either intoned by a cantor or said, while the choir respond with the usual 'Hear our prayer', 'Lord, graciously hear us', or whatever. The choir then vocalize the final chord in four-part harmony as a background over which the next petition comes, and so on. Sung discreetly this can be most effective and in no way a gimmick providing it is not embarked on too frequently.

Responsories

The problems surrounding psalmody were discussed earlier. A similar way of coping with responsorial petitions and responses, apart from the Eucharist, is for a clutch of verses to be sung to which the congregation can add a suitable refrain which underlines the mood. But the refrain must be easy for the congregation to cope with, not like one I heard where the people came to grief every time at the C ♮ and B ♭

(see Example 9.3). Had they been asked to sing C# and B ♮ the feel for the key centre would have been maintained and no difficulties would have arisen. What we experienced on that occasion was unexpected, and an inevitable pitfall for the average member of a congregation.

Example 9.3

In our new forms of service more opportunities than ever are emerging for corporate involvement in various ways as distinct from the more familiar versicles and responses mentioned earlier. In this, clergy, choirs, congregations, even organs and other instruments, could all have a distinctive role to play.

Contemporary Trends

I make no excuse here for re-emphasizing some of what I said earlier and which I believe to be of importance.

The first signs of departure from long-established norms and traditions were seen, not surprisingly, in hymnody which inescapably affects all concerned with public worship. As mentioned earlier, what was to develop into radical changes in both words and music was heralded in the 1950s with the emergence of the Twentieth Century Church Light Music Group in which Patrick Appleford and Geoffrey Beaumont were significant in writing tunes which caught on at the time. J. R. Watson sums it up when he maintains that 'There has been a lot that has been earnest, but not much that has been enjoyable or inspirational.'[1] Appleford and Beaumont, and their coterie, wrote in a style reminiscent of Noel Coward and Ivor Novello (who in secular terms wrote much better music). The jazzy tune Beaumont wrote for 'O Jesus, I have promised' is marginally more apt than the dull tune so long associated with these words, though the same cannot in any way be said for Appleford's ALTON which he wrote for 'Firmly I believe and truly' and which to my mind debases through its triviality the superb words of Cardinal Newman.

The Beaumont/Appleford group found a ready niche in schools. This was probably because they were, in the early 1960s, writing in a then novel mould which on the face of it was more appealing in school assemblies than many of the more four-square traditional hymn tunes. But it was not only among the young that this music found favour; for many middle-aged people this was so reminiscent of the Fred Astaire and Ginger Rogers type of dance music which in a secular world fitted the popular bill. Perhaps Bertram Barnby hit the nail on the head when he suggested that 'the group made the fatal mistake of setting their tunes to well-known words that had much-loved tunes of their own'.[2] One of the most successful of the Appleford hymns is, as we saw earlier (pages 24–5), 'Jesus, humble was your birth'. This, together with Sydney Carter's 'The Lord of the Dance', has found a place in most of today's hymn books, assured through their credibility in being teaching hymns.

Appleford also wrote a simple folk-style setting for what at that time was called the Series 3 Communion Service. As with so many innovators what he and his colleagues did served to pave the way towards consolidating new thinking done in the event so much better by those who followed on who have developed to advantage the spadework of their predecessors. The real problem with so much of the music of that era, which sadly to a large extent still persists today, is that effectually the music took priority over the words, allowing them only secondary significance.

Before long the charismatic renewal movement caught on in England, with much of its initial impetus and thrust coming from the multiplicity of like-minded denominations in North America and later in the Far East. This has resulted in the evangelical wing now being the fastest growing area of the Church of England. Its specialized brand of theological thinking and teaching, with plenty of assurance, but far less plausible acceptance of other viewpoints, has produced a tendency to arrogance which at its worst brands dissenters as second-class Christians. Why it has taken such a hold on young and old alike, even whole families, is not within the province of this book, though it does beg the question as to what there is in it which provides such a magnet for so many.

The associated non-traditional music is obviously a contributory factor and in many churches is fast becoming the norm, and dangerously exclusive with its emphasis on choruses and worship songs. Much of it is for unison voices, often with the use of instruments other than the organ. This in itself is no bad innovation for it mirrors much of the musical work experienced in schools, which can be a bonus in worship. A further bonus is that it is invariably chosen, prepared and rehearsed with a degree of commitment and care which cannot be said to apply to all traditional areas. If only the music were of better quality and of more substance than the invariably trite phrases repeated *ad nauseam*. Much of the prevailing music is made the more dreary by being in the minor key, exerting a monotonous and all but hypnotic influence. Ironically, one of the favourite clichés is the awkward and affected application of syncopation, as in Example 10.1.

Example 10.1

Praise to the Lord_

This is not easy to sing accurately, though maybe approximation with an element of improvisation is what is required, as in Example 10.2, taken from 'Our God reigns' with music by Leonard Smith Jnr.

On the other hand, there is surely a real danger when clergy and others see the musical involvement of all and sundry in pastoral terms, whatever their degree of expertise. This brings into question standards, which are perhaps

Example 10.2

*reigns!*_____ *Our God reigns!*_____ *Our God reigns!*

perceived as of lesser importance than the need to involve people musically. If so, this is far removed from the generally held concept that worship in all its constituents should be the very best we can offer, not least in standards. Once we start to depart from the need to pursue – and maintain – high standards we are on the downward slippery slope, however much some will try to persuade us that the pursuit of excellence in church – though not necessarily in our daily mode of life and living – should be written off as a relic of a bygone age and ethos. Also, standards are surely as much for the edification of those on the receiving end as they are for the musicians.

One of the saddest situations to have emerged in our time is that in many churches there is an almost total rejection of the musical past and its traditions, something mirrored very much in the secular life of the nation. This is particularly in evidence in those churches where traditional hymns are seldom, if ever, sung. On the other side of the coin, how much potential is unrealized when statements such as 'Jesus loves me, I love Jesus' are repeated again and again in a deadpan way. A statement such as this is fundamental to the Christian faith, but how much more meaningful if it were

'Je-sus loves me – I love Jes-sus'

with each repetition the more emphatic, together with varying dynamics and perhaps an alternation between higher and
lower voices, or between children and adults. In this way this
typical simple phrase can be made more of.

We can only conclude that although music may be highly
rated in evangelical and renewed churches, how it is performed is not always given a high priority. Perhaps we might
take a leaf out of the book of the Crystal Cathedral in
California where some hundreds of musicians, ranging from
choirs and orchestras to handbell ringers, are involved each
week in music-making of a high calibre. Although this may
be a unique example there are many other churches where
continuing high standards are the target and where the worship is much enhanced as a result.

What the renewal churches can do is to teach the congregations and choirs of the more traditional establishments to
look, and maybe even feel, happy. Although many of us of
the older generation were brought up to be serious in church,
times have changed – and a smiling countenance will help
produce a warmer tone when singing. I well remember a tele-
vised 'Songs of Praise' some years ago featuring West Indians
in the Southwark Diocese. They looked so happy, smiled as
they sang and were not averse to a degree of bodily movement. This was admirable given the type of music they were
engaged in, although it would hardly be suitable for a penitential seventeenth-century anthem. Even so, the fact remains
that many 'traditional' Anglicans are by nature staid and
unwilling to show emotions when in church, while others go
over the top. There could surely be a modicum of displayed
feeling to good effect.

Some of today's more liberal music does not always fare as
well as it might in comparison with Sankey and Moody who
wrote texts which told a story and had a sense of purpose.
The music had thrust, often with a refrain at the end of each
verse, as with many of the best of the Salvation Army hymns.

The Victorians were confident – sometimes super-confident; they knew where they were going, and they got there, and not only in church music. The one failing was in the overloading of sentimentality, both in much of the music itself and in the way it was performed, as we noted earlier with regard to Mendelssohn and Stainer. If the text is weak, uninspired, and even banal, what hope is there for the music even when amplified to excess? There is a limit to what you can do when so much relies on fragmented repetitiveness.

For many years Diocesan Choral Festivals and similar events have provided annual occasions for choirs to sing *en masse*. If you happen to be the solitary tenor in a village choir, the thrill of being with twenty or thirty tenors in a choir of some hundreds singing in a great cathedral is a shot in the arm as well as being a learning process. I have known singers dine out for a long time, and with pride, on how inspiring and memorable such occasions are, with perhaps a large-scale anthem being specially learned for the occasion which a choir may never have the opportunity, or the resources, to sing again on their own. In my RSCM days I twice conducted the Ely Diocesan Choirs Festival in King's College Chapel, Cambridge, where it has been said that even a sneeze sounds musical. In rehearsal I would tell the choirs to listen at the end of a loud piece to the echo and to look up at the magnificence of the architecture, for the two are interlocked.

Various factors such as the cost today of transporting choirs maybe considerable distances, the shortage of singers through the demise of many traditional choirs, and the active discouragement of some of the clergy, have made considerable inroads in recent years into the feasibility of these events. Their place has in some measure been taken by occasions such as 'Prom Praise' in the Royal Albert Hall. These to an extent draw in individual singers more than choirs, and lack the learning opportunity which is so invaluable a part of choral festivals. With these comes a large and skilled orchestra, much crowd noise, and near hysterical cheering with the waving of Union flags making it seem like a religious Last Night of the Proms. Everyone certainly seems to be enjoying themselves which is fair enough, though this cannot be termed worship in the accepted sense, but no doubt the promoters would contest this. The process is undemanding and fails to 'get to grips with the doctrine of the Church', as Richard Watson once put it. Hearing 'Nimrod' from Elgar's Enigma Variations sung to religious words surely puts the cart before the horse and becomes an intrusion. Why – and to what effect?

'Songs of Praise', the BBC Sunday evening religious programme, has greatly changed in concept and production in recent years, becoming in the process more and more variable in content, no doubt in a well-intentioned effort to please all persuasions. Musically, tunes which have been reharmonized not only lose their character but are dismissive of what the composer wrote. An element of cheapness and playing to the gallery can result in bizarre tempi, such as 'Onward, Christian soldiers' being subjected to a very brisk two-in-a-bar, turning it into something akin to a two-step; while 'My song is love unknown' has been presented as a brisk two-in-a-bar with a young lady crooning the tune in a way which flagrantly distorts John Ireland's spacious music so that virtually every vestige of the original is lost. Playing to the gallery in this and other ways such as extravagent musical introductions and sudden key changes between one verse and another does a grave disservice to words and music alike.

Conductors, mercifully seldom on camera, flay their arms around in extravagant gestures as if it were the finale of Beethoven's Choral Symphony. Most hymns are conducted with an unvarying jerky beat whatever the mood of the hymn, to which the singers respond by equally accentuating every word or syllable, such as 'Blest are the pure in heart'. Sir John Barbirolli maintained that the smaller the beat the more the musicians will respond, simply because they have to listen and watch the more carefully. A cynical, though realistic, conclusion is that 'Songs of Praise' is sadly too often an example of how not to do things, though from time to time there are exceptions.

Today the Church in its various denominations has by and large settled on two distinct, if obvious, directions in its music, the traditional and the not so traditional. Both have their virtues and both their dangers. While present-day hymnody was discussed in Chapter 3 and earlier in this chapter, in terms of anthems and settings of the Communion service a major significant factor has been the influence of John Rutter who has seldom trod a completely traditional path but who never fails to bring a new and welcome fresh look to whatever he embarks on. The popularity of his music was assured from the time that he first came up with Christmas carols, either original or in arrangements in which he was admirably partnered by David Willcocks whose arrangements of 'O come, all ye faithful', 'Hark the herald angels sing' and 'Once in royal David's city' rightly continue to retain their popularity against all comers, so much so that Christmas for many would not be complete without the music of Rutter and Willcocks.

What singles out Rutter? First and foremost it is his ever-ingenious originality. Virtually no two of his works are alike in terms of melodic, harmonic or rhythmic content, and he has a never-failing integrity which singles him out as a significant craftsman with a distinctive hallmark as easily recognizable as that of Vaughan Williams. He is, moreover, a practical musician as witness the many recordings he has conducted and the number of concerts he directs both here and abroad. He has also emerged in recent years as a scholarly editor as can be seen from the Oxford University

Press catalogue. Much of his music is within the capabilities of the average musician, certainly in vocal demands if not quite so readily in terms of some of his accompaniments. Even though considerable rehearsal may be needed, the end product is within the grasp of most musicians and as stimulating and rewarding for the listener as for the performer. In the annals of composition he will go down as someone who projected a new and often exciting approach to church music and, in doing so, has blown away a lot of cobwebs.

Rutter's imaginative and engaging approach to his extensive carol output is a special example of the breadth and invention of his versatile musicianship and how he can turn his hand in an original, but always sensible, way in providing music which excels in the three necessary virtues of acceptable melody, harmony and rhythm. His powers of invention are such that no two of his carols are alike.

Although Rutter has a special place in the English music of today he is by no means alone. Francis Jackson, Richard Shephard and Philip Moore – the York trilogy – Martin How, Anthony Piccolo, Richard Lloyd, John Sanders, Andrew Carter and Colin Mawby are among a clutch of composers to have emerged in recent years and who continue to flourish. All in their different ways have advantageously widened the repertoire with music attractive to amateurs and professionals alike.

A fundamental feature of the liturgical revolution of recent years has been the updating and use of language in contemporary terms for what are seen as the needs of today. While some composers are readily attracted to the new texts, others genuinely find them a disincentive, claiming they are difficult to set, even impossible. Is it perhaps a matter of familiarity and a consequent feeling of ease with the old wording, or maybe an attitude which sometimes verges on bigotry? After all, many traditional composers have set W. H. Auden and

T. S. Eliot without compunction – and neither wrote in seventeenth-century language.

In drawing together the strands, the situation basically is probably not much different today than at any other time when change within the Church has been a pertinent, if at times divisive, issue. It was ever thus. The Church of England has always sought to cater for all needs in its strands of churchmanship – evangelical, centre of the road and Anglo-Catholic alike. While today this has in musical terms more or less concentrated on the issues discussed earlier in this chapter and elsewhere, the premise is that what works and is suitable to one situation may be entirely out of place and unsuitable to another. To quote St Paul, 'There are diversities of gifts, but the same Spirit.' Ultimately, quality, both in the music we elect to use and the standards adopted in performing it, is mandatory. This cannot be over-stressed, if only because it is not always afforded a high priority. However much people may try to dissuade us against this, standards and quality are nevertheless linked yard-sticks. These must be constantly scrutinized, maintained, and improved if music in worship is to be of value and worth – an enrichment, a bonus, but never an embarrassment.

In concluding these thoughts on the effects that some trends are having on our church music, two quotations seem relevant. First, Herbert Howells, writing in *English Church Music* as far back as 1966, saw the dangers of resorting to a 'cheap surrender to popularity'.[3] And Bertram Barnby maintains that: 'With so rich and varied a heritage at our disposal, there can be no excuse for the perpetuation of the second-rate, or for the over-use on one hand, or the total, exclusion on the other, of the music of any particular period or style.'[4]

11

Epilogue-Recapitulation

In much the same way that the eternal truths of the Christian faith need to be constantly in our thoughts, the more so in the semi-pagan world we inhabit, similar emphases in terms of the Church's music need to be constantly restated and highlighted.

To realize the full impact of the music, be it sacred, secular, vocal or instrumental, phrasing is of the essence. Too often in church music this does not seem to enter into the equation as the priority it should be, certainly in terms of hymnody. It may be stating the obvious to say that because music is a mobile art, phrasing must be a prior concern if what we hear is to make any rational artistic sense. The same criterion applies to any form of public speaking, but even more so when words are given an added dimension by being clothed with music. And, incidentally, how important the spoken parts are to the completeness and integrity of a church service, and how crucial the role of a choir in leading with clear articulation those parts of a service which are corporate. A choir cannot opt out of the non-musical parts, for worship is an inclusive responsibility, not merely a musical one.

To illustrate phrasing take a simple melody such as that in Example 11.1, a useful parallel being the rise and fall of a group of hills:

Example 11.1

The black notes provide the mobility while the dotted minim needs to grow in intensity and become the climax both in its length and as the high point in pitch. Given these constraints the phrase becomes *espressivo* or, to use another musical label, romantic, for surely most music is in essence romantic – the term is not necessarily applicable only to one particular, often German, nineteenth-century aspect. A good string player would automatically and without question play the phrase in this way as a matter of course. Sadly this sometimes escapes the church choir. S A T B music is in a way akin to a string quartet with each voice part listening not only to themselves but even more to the other three parts if 100 per cent accuracy in chording and balance is to be achieved. Singers and string players have to make their own notes, unlike the ready-made keyboard, *and* they can only do this through listening. Linked closely with this is the exciting fact mentioned in the introductory chapter that music is the one art form which is dead notes on a page until the interpreter brings them to life. What an onus – and what an exciting privilege – this is, and one replete with interpretative possibilities.

Choirs constantly need to be cognizant of accuracy in vowel sounds and consonants which are the two key constituents which form words, vowels as the tone makers and consonants providing the articulation. A typical example is 'praise', which phonetically is 'per-ay-ee-ze', with a double consonant at the outset (pr), then a dipthong (ae) and then a robust consonant (z).

Finally, here are some factors stressed earlier, which need to be constantly underlined:

1. The necessity to relay **mood**. The Crucifixus in Bach's Mass in B minor is a very different proposition from the simplicity with which Merbecke set the same words in his Creed. Though both express the same sentiments they are poles apart in mood and approach. How seldom do choirs and organists relay the solemnity of these words when singing Merbecke.

2. **Conducting.** How essential it is to be both sparing and discreet if only to avoid visually distracting the congregation. There are many instances where the music will flow more readily by beating one-in-a-bar in duple and triple time, and two rather than four. The momentum of the music should be the deciding factor.

3. The importance of **hymns**. They involve *all* concerned with music in worship and are integral to most services. We need continually to be aware of the fact that for many of the congregation this is their sole musical contribution, and it is the tune and not the words which provide the memorability, often through association.

4. The acoustics of a building must to a large extent determine the **tempo**. While a fairly brisk speed when indicated will suit a normal size church, a steadier and more marked approached is called for in a large and perhaps resonant building.

5. The responsibility of the organist, or an instrumental group, in providing colour in the **accompaniment**. Much of the music of John Rutter bears this out as do organ accompaniments of orchestral scores such as excerpts from Brahms' *Requiem*.

6. Too often church musicians tend to veer towards one **style**, and one only, whatever the music. While Tye's 'O come, ye servants of the Lord' needs a sustained legato

treatment, this is poles apart from what underlines Britten's highly emotive and brittle Jubilate. The ability to relay the style in which each piece of music is cast is essential, though the reverse side of this particular coin is seen when clergy and others maintain that God is not being properly worshipped unless everything musical is fast – and loud. It follows that the correct dimension and mood of each and every piece of music must be sensed from the outset and relayed to the forces involved.

Ultimately, what we do must come from the heart. Although our efforts may be technically and stylistically correct we must, as the motto of the RSCM reminds us, sing both with the spirit and with the understanding, otherwise the words will not be beautified nor enriched.

While evidence today may point to the evangelical and renewal churches being in the ascendancy, we need to take stock as to why they attract so many in the younger age groups. Maybe the associated music is a factor, much of it reflecting that of the secular world. If this is so perhaps it points to the need for those more traditionally orientated to guide the young towards the more lasting benefits that quality music can bring for the betterment of worship. After all, the young are the forerunners, as many of us of the older generation hopefully were in our time. It is not either or, so much as both and.

For the future, if worship has no constituent of mystery or awe gleaned from the best of the past, something crucial will be lacking, and this applies as much to the music as to anything else. The transcendent extends far beyond this material world.

In conclusion, I hope this book will be of some help to all who are involved with the role of music in worship which demands the very best we can offer in every aspect. This in its turn brings enrichment to those on the receiving end and a sense of purpose for the musicians. The age-old tradition of music as a unique means of beautifying and enriching the words used in worship is a crucial one which must be safe-guarded and upheld.

What a challenge lies before us for the future!

Notes

Chapter 1

1. Paul Spicer: *Herbert Howells*, p. 133.
2. Bertram L. Barnby: *In Concert Sing*, p. 174.
3. Kenneth Clark: *Civilisation*, p. 243.

Chapter 3

1. Barnby: *In Concert Sing*, p. 27.
2. Ibid., p. 38.
3. J. R. Watson: *The English Hymn*, p. ix.

Chapter 6

1. Christopher Palmer: *Herbert Howells. A centenary celebration*, p. 86.
2. Kenneth R. Long: *The Music of the English Church*, p. 374.
3. Ibid., p. 371.
4. Palmer: *Herbert Howells*, p. 135.
5. Ibid., p. 15.
6. Ibid., p. 133.

Chapter 7

1. E. H. Fellowes: *English Cathedral Music*, p. 103.
2. Long: *The Music of the English Church*, p. 310.

3. Fellowes: *English Cathedral Music*, p. 224.
4. Spicer: *Herbert Howells*, p. 135.
5. Fellowes: *English Cathedral Music*, p. 246.

Chapter 9

1. Long: *The Music of the English Church*, p. 25.

Chapter 10

1. Watson: *The English Hymn*, p. 531.
2. Barnby: *In Concert Sing*, p. 174.
3. Spicer: *Herbert Howells*, p. 134.
4. Barnby: *In Concert Sing*, p. 176.

Index

Hymns

Hymn Tunes